Celia Thaxter
SELECTED WRITINGS

Julia Older

(for Celia)

Celia Thaxter
SELECTED WRITINGS

Edited and Introduced by
Julia Older

APPLEDORE BOOKS
Hancock NH 03449-0174

The material included in Celia Thaxter Selected Writings is from original
nineteenth century texts:
  Among the Isles of Shoals James B Osgood & Co. 1873
  The Poems of Celia Thaxter, Appledore Edition   Roland Thaxter 1896
  An Island Garden Celia Thaxter & Houghton, Mifflin 1894
  Letters Houghton, Mifflin 1895
  Stories and Poems for Children Houghton, Mifflin 1895
  A Memorable Murder The Atlantic Monthly 1861

Permission granted by:
  The National Museum of American Art, Smithsonian Institution.
  Gift of John Gellatly.
  Cover reproduction of painting by Childe Hassam.
  "In the Garden" Oil on canvas, 1892.

For permission to reprint material which accompanies these selections
contact: Appledore Books, Hancock NH 03449-0174.

HG Graphic Design, Alstead NH
Printed in 12 point Times
by Book Press, Inc.
Brattleboro VT
United States of America

ISBN 0-9627162-4-3
Library of Congress Catalog Card Number: 97-71061

First Edition

Dedicated to the Memory of
LOUISE DALRYMPLE OLDER

CONTENTS

INTRODUCTION

Louisa May Alcott, Emily Dickinson, and Celia Thaxter were contemporaneous New England writers. Many of us have read *LITTLE WOMEN* and can quote a line of Emily's poems. But who was Celia Thaxter?

Morning Glories and Sea Roses

She was born in Portsmouth, New Hampshire, June 29, 1835. Her father was a New Hampshire state senator, a Portsmouth selectman, and editor at the *Portsmouth Herald*. Celia was four when Thomas and Eliza Laighton packed lock, stock, and barrel and took her on a steamer to White Island nine miles out to sea. Thomas had applied for Postmaster of Portsmouth and when he was passed over he continued as temporary keeper of White Island Light. Ever resourceful, and with an eye to starting a commercial fishing business, he purchased four of the nine Isles of Shoals.

During the first December on White Island a fierce storm swept away the catwalk from their humble stone cottage to the lighthouse, along with the rowboats and everything else not anchored to the granite ledges. A pilot boat was scheduled to bring provisions and whale oil once a month, but that winter the crossing was far too dangerous and months passed without their seeing another soul.

While mainland girls played with ceramic dolls and learned proper etiquette, Celia lived a different life. She helped her father polish the huge red and gold lantern globes, trimmed the wicks, and rubbed the salt spray from the lighthouse windows. Migrating song birds often flew into the lighted lanterns on their way up the coast; she collected their small bodies to bury in graves adorned with twisted morning glories and sea roses. At low tide she walked the milk cow to Seavy Island, which was connected to White Island by an exposed isthmus, scrambling barefoot over the pebbles and tidal pools to the grass on the other side.

Although for the most part Celia grew up in isolation, her education was far from neglected. Home schooling was the norm in those days and during raw winter evenings she read Shakespeare and Tennyson aloud to her proud parents and her baby brothers Oscar and Cedric. Perhaps because of this insularity, a strong bond with her parents and brothers endured.

In 1841 the Laightons moved to Haley's house on Smutty-Nose Island. The late Samuel Haley had built a salt works, set up windmills to grind grain, planted an orchard, and built a sea wall financed by four bars of pirate silver he'd found on Smutty-Nose. In this house the Laightons finally could spread out and enjoy the luxury of not bumping into each other.

Thomas had been elected to the New Hampshire House, and while he was at the New Hampshire capitol in Concord his wife Eliza took in boarders. Numbering among their summer guests was Thomas Higginson, an enthusiastic young liberal attracted to women and women's writing. Like many, he was charmed by Celia's precocity, giving her books and encouraging her growing interest in poetry. (Higginson went on to become a literary critic, essayist, and a fleeting friend to Emily Dickinson.) One summer Richard Dana, author of *TWO YEARS BEFORE THE MAST,* sat at the Laighton table along with John Weiss and Levi Thaxter, recent Harvard graduates, and Levi's sister Lucy. Also present were Lizzie, the sister of the celebrated poet John Greenleaf Whittier, and Margie Curzon. Although only thirteen, Celia fitted right in, and all of them soon became fast friends. When Weiss, a brilliant theologian, and Thaxter, an eloquent dramatist, weren't grandstanding for the girls' attention, the young people sailed, rambled, and roved the Isles of Shoals.

Sweet Talk and the Pretty Miranda

A few years later, Celia moved to Appledore, the largest of the Isles of Shoals where Thomas Laighton and Mr. Thaxter Sr., were building a large new resort hotel. James Russell

Lowell, editor of *The Atlantic Monthly*, opened the doors of Appledore House on June 15, 1848. While the parents were involved with the hotel, Levi Thaxter, Jr., tutored the Laighton children. Oscar and Cedric frequently played hooky, being more interested in their own lucrative summer lobster business than learning Latin verbs. This left impressionable fourteen-year-old Celia alone with the tall bearded man eleven years more versed in the ways of the world. Levi, who aspired to a career in the theatre, could persuade a green lobster into a pot of boiling water, and he quickly sweet-talked the naive young girl into marrying him. Learning of the romance, the Laightons sent the ardent suitor packing and enrolled their daughter at the Mount Washington Female Seminary in Boston, hoping she would come to her senses.

But the separation only fueled the fire, and on September 30, 1851, Celia and Levi were married on Appledore Island.

The first year of marriage was a happy one for the newlyweds. Levi was ecstatic when Nathaniel Hawthorne paid them a visit. But it was Celia who captivated the renowned author of THE SCARLET LETTER, and in his AMERICAN NOTEBOOKS Hawthorne remembers her as "the pretty Miranda."

Levi was hired to teach and preach in a one-room chapel which doubled as a school on Star Island. Levi's Sunday services were more like poetry readings and plays than sermons. Nevertheless, the fishing families adored the couple and were thrilled when Celia gave birth to Karl Laighton Thaxter, the first child born on the Shoals in nearly a hundred years.

Cooking, Cleaning, and Poetry

One fateful day Celia's life capsized like the boat she watched in horror from the shore. Her brother and husband had gone sailing, and in a sudden squall overturned, and miraculously washed onto the rocks. They were unharmed, but from that moment on Levi vowed they would live on the mainland. Celia, pregnant with her second son John, grudgingly left the Shoals and settled in a rented house in Newtonville, Massachusetts.

They were still there four years later when Roland was born. By then it had become apparent that seven-year-old Karl was a backward, tantrum-ridden child lagging far behind his younger brothers. Celia devoted as much time as she could to her "poor little spud." One day she read Karl a poem she had dashed off line by line between cooking, cleaning, and spur-of-the-moment guests. She had been homesick for her mother and the Shoals and expressed that longing in "Land-locked." A few months later she picked up an issue of *The Atlantic Monthly* to see if anyone she knew was published in it. She had met Harriet Beecher Stowe and Henry Longfellow and was thrilled whenever coming across their work in the prominent national magazine. Reading through *The Atlantic*, Celia stopped at a familiar poem and in disbelief stared at the title, "Land-locked." She hadn't submitted it. Who had? Not Karl; he could barely write his own name and address. Levi and her brothers categorically denied having sent it, and Celia eventually gave up trying to find the culprit.

Bolstered by seeing her poem in print, she gathered the other poems she had written and offered them to James Fields, the new editor of *The Atlantic Monthly*. Fields not only printed more of Celia's poems but also introduced her to the literary luminaries of Boston, including the popular British novelist Charles Dickens who was in town for a reading. At an intimate dinner party hosted by the Fields, the colorful author of DAVID COPPERFIELD and A CHRISTMAS CAROL was enchanted by Celia and her pirate and ghost stories, urging her to write them down. The next morning he confided to Annie Fields that he was so taken with Celia he had dreamt about her.

In 1872 Levi arranged for the publication of his wife's first poetry collection. Celia also worked on stories and essays about the Shoals. For like Louisa May Alcott (who submitted to some of the same magazines) Celia now was supporting her family with her writing. Levi refused to work at his father's law office and wasn't steadily employed. He abandoned Celia and Karl at the Newtonville house. Ostensibly following doctor's orders, he headed for warmer climes with his two sons, guns, and camping gear. He was gone for months.

Enter John Greenleaf Whittier

As Celia's reputation as a writer grew, so did her self-confidence in other aspects of her life. She summered on the Shoals without Levi, helping her aging parents run the 300-room resort hotel. In turn, they built their daughter a cottage where she could write and invite a widening circle of literary and artistic friends.

Among them figured preeminent poet John Greenleaf Whittier. Fearing that Levi might commit Karl to a mental institution, Celia sought advice from Whittier, who was active in the reform of New England mental institutions. The soft-spoken Quaker took a personal interest in Karl, and Celia was grateful. The eligible sixty-year-old bachelor and thirty-three-year-old married woman thoroughly enjoyed each other's company. John encouraged Celia's writing; she listened to his passionate discourses on abolition.

During this time menacing guns from coastal military camps could be heard on the Shoals, and though Celia usually left politics to the men, Whittier had aroused her social consciousness. "Minute Guns" and "The Great Blue Heron: A Warning" are but two of a number of protest poems she wrote in the wake of the Civil War.

By 1868 Celia was corresponding with John on a regular basis. "Do you know you looked so finely, so full of life and of power," she wrote after his summer-long visit to the Shoals. "All my heart was stirred looking up at you, thinking of you and all you have done. —Great heaven, what eyes you have . . ." This is not a platonic letter by any stretch of the imagination, and although Whittier requested they burn their correspondence, the letters that do survive suggest their deep affection for one another.

Murder, She Wrote

One moonlit March midnight in 1873 a desperate transient, Louis Wagner, pushed a skiff into the ocean at Portsmouth, rowed nine miles to Smutty-Nose, stole a dollar plus change, brutally axed two young women, and rowed back to the mainland. Reporters and investigators hounded the Laighton family since one of the murdered women had been in their employ. And gawking strangers did everything in their power to bribe Shoalers to row them to the scene of the crime.

The Shoals had been a refuge for Celia, endowing her with a love of nature and offering a safe haven unfettered by mainland concerns. That bond of trust and security irrevocably changed.

The brutal deaths were followed by the natural passing of Celia's mother, and to overcome her grief she launched into several writing projects, including the often reprinted

"A Memorable Murder" for *The Atlantic Monthly.* She took up painting and surrounded herself with close friends at her Appledore parlor, but misfortune continued. In 1877 Celia found the body of artist William Morris Hunt in a shallow pool near her cottage. She had known her friend was depressed when she invited him to the Shoals, but the suicide shocked Celia and close friends. Rather than lapse into depression herself, however, she writes, "Oh, how grand he looked when we laid him down and let him rest at last. Beautiful dear fellow! We could not keep away from him; he was fascinating even in death."

Portholes

In the 1880s Celia's brother Cedric fell in love and married. Oscar too was smitten but had been refused, and deprived of a honeymoon, he accompanied his sister to Europe. Celia delighted in the Italian countryside and blue of the Mediterranean. Infused with energy and spirit, she took painting lessons in Boston on her return. Before long her painting teacher, Childe Hassam, fell under Celia's spell, and she whisked the up-and-coming artist to her island salon where he set up his easel beneath the hop vines. He painted the garden, the parlor, the rocks, the sparkling sea— and Celia. The white-haired woman carries her matronly stature proudly as she poses in the shade on the piazza and in her garden. Hassam readily agreed to paint the illustrations for her book AN ISLAND GARDEN, and because of Thaxter's vision and support, it was no longer necessary for him to eke out a living as an illustrator. Childe Hassam's oils and watercolors of the Shoals helped to win him an immediate and permanent place in the pantheon of American Impressionists.

Meanwhile, Levi stopped gallivanting and purchased a sea captain's house on Kittery Point in Maine with an unobstructed view of the Isles of Shoals. Perhaps the Champernowne House, as it was called, was a conciliatory gift from the negligent husband, who by then was gravely ill. He died in 1884. Celia and Karl took rooms for the winter at a Boston hotel where Whittier was staying.

Neuralgic Swords and Champagne

With her parents gone and one brother married, the management of the Appledore Hotel fell upon Celia's shoulders, weighting her down with work. She continued to write for a living and sold china which she hand-painted. Exhausted from worry about Karl, the constant work at the hotel, and a restless spirit, Celia experienced serious illness for the first time in her life.

Plagued with attacks of neuralgia, she was given morphine injections to relieve the pain in her chest. Forgetting demands of the hotel and resting an entire summer gave her time to read and reflect. When her mother died, Celia had dabbled in spiritism and consulted mediums. Now faced by her own mortality, she explored theosophy and the Eastern thought of Mohini, then residing in Boston. "I am become a most humble and devoted follower of Christ, our Christ," she writes Whittier, "for all races have their own Christ to save and help them." The long letter closes with a discussion of reincarnation and the laws of karma.

Revived by rest and awakened to a powerful new belief in God and the universe, Celia gloried in her grandchildren, friends, and garden, but increasingly she took to her bed. In one letter she mentions the doctor has prescribed champagne, a cure that amused and agreed with her. But her health continued to decline.

Celia Thaxter died August 26, 1894, on the sofa of her Appledore parlor shortly before sunrise.

From Obscurity into the Light

Celia's was an era of fanciful epithets. To the adoring public she was the Rose of the Isles, and Sarah Orne Jewett, the Princess of Berwick. Both were popular and their work recognized. But as gas lamps were replaced by electricity and typesetting by Linotype, the books of these singular writers collected dust on library shelves.

Although a volume of Emily Dickinson's poems appeared in 1890, she too languished in literary obscurity until a 1955 collection was published, and seemingly overnight the Belle of Amherst became the White Goddess of American poetry. Louisa May Alcott's LITTLE WOMEN was widely acclaimed and remained in print. However, only now are her other novels and stories available. Sarah Orne Jewett also has been rediscovered, and her exquisite story collection COUNTRY OF THE POINTED FIRS may be found in the "classics" section of most book stores.

But what about Celia Thaxter, decidedly an extraordinary woman and writer ahead of her time who:

Founded the first artist colony in America and
   championed American greats—Hawthorne,
   Childe Hassam, the MacDowells and others.
Shunned convention, separated from her husband,
   and forged a writing career in an era when few
   women took such risks.
Raised their backward son single-handedly.
Wrote a beloved garden book that has become a
   national classic.
Contributed an enduring legacy of writings to
   future generations.

Alcott, Dickinson, Jewett and Thaxter all refused to shackle themselves to the confining strictures of Victorian New England. Yet Thaxter is the only one missing from the OXFORD COMPANION TO WOMEN'S WRITING IN AMERICA.

Celia Thaxter doesn't fit into a regional framework, but she is inextricably bound to place. With the best nature writers she expands her few island acres into a boundless world of wonder. Much in the same way Henry Beston's THE OUTERMOST HOUSE binds him to Cape Cod and Margery Stoneman Douglas' RIVER OF GRASS makes her a part of the Everglades, Celia Thaxter always will be associated with the Isles of Shoals.

Selected Writings

The six major works represented in this compilation of Celia Thaxter's writing include excerpts from: *AMONG THE ISLES OF SHOALS*, *COLLECTED VERSE*, *AN ISLAND GARDEN*, *LETTERS*, *STORIES*, and *A MEMORABLE MURDER*. These selections reflect Celia's versatility and are an introduction to many facets of her lifework.

AMONG THE ISLES OF SHOALS describes in a painterly way the natural seascape and historical island backdrop of Celia's cherished home. This, her first book of prose, was so popular it was reprinted and sold in train stations as a travel guide— few travel books are so immediate and captivating.

POEMS have been culled from Thaxter's *COLLECTED VERSE* and are presented not necessarily in the order she wrote them but to underline important chronological events in Celia's personal life. Her friend, Sarah Orne Jewett, noted in the preface to this posthumous collection that Celia's poems comprise "something like a journal of her life and thought."

AN ISLAND GARDEN offers the prose of a seasoned author writing for a larger audience. In the modern idiom, this volume might be labeled a "how-to gardening book." But few gardening books are so lively, descriptive, and delightful. Childe Hassam's evocative illustrations which accompany the volume are the proverbial icing on the cake. Today, this book may be found in the private libraries of gardeners across America.

The *LETTERS* were collected by Annie Fields (wife of the editor of *The Atlantic Monthly*) and Rose Lamb, another of Celia's many friends and correspondents. For the most part these confidential intimate letters present an irresistible mixture of domestic detail, literary gossip, and elevated discourse. Celia lets down her hair and shares her most intimate secrets.

The *STORIES* were submitted to children's publications early in Thaxter's career and compiled posthumously in *POEMS & STORIES FOR CHILDREN* (1895). Celia had three small children and her interaction with them triggered fond and humorous memories of her own carefree childhood. As with all of Celia's work, the Shoals create a backdrop for these charming innocent tales.

A MEMORABLE MURDER has been reprinted several times since it first appeared in *The Atlantic Monthly* in 1873. The article was written on speculation, that is, Celia took the initiative to write it without knowing if she would be paid for her considerable effort. Readers unfamiliar with the gruesome chain of events will find this gripping account difficult to put down.

Each of these selections is prefaced with comments about what was going on in Celia's lifetime as well as information about the publication of the work. Friends and colleagues often encouraged Celia in her writing, and the role they played is elaborated.

Readability has been a prime objective in editing these nineteenth century works for a modern audience. Page-long Jamesian paragraphs are repunctuated so that readers may catch their breath. The poems no longer have widows (dangling ends of lines the printer couldn't fit on the page), and a few other printing typos have been corrected. Today, these are changes a copy editor would address before publication. But in Celia's day a great many variables were involved, starting with the legibility of the author's handwriting and ending with the proficiency of the typesetter.

The entries are labeled and clearly formatted so that readers can identify the substance and subject matter of the excerpt. In AMONG THE ISLES OF SHOALS new subjects are introduced by paragraphs. In the other selections, spaces indicate where one excerpt ends and the next begins.

These selections offer a taste of the information, imagery and insights crammed into Celia Thaxter's books. I hope they engage you enough to look for the originals, reprints, and biographies—and relish them cover to cover.

—Julia Older

AMONG THE
ISLES OF SHOALS

Preface

James Fields, who had published Celia's poems in *The Atlantic Monthly*, suggested she draft some prose about the Isles of Shoals which he could print for the literary magazine. But the young mother of three rambunctious boys was hard-pressed to find the time, and in October 1862 Celia writes Fields from her Newtonville home: "I'm sorry I've as yet no prosaic manuscript for you. Just as soon as this family is settled for the winter so that every wheel doesn't creak in despair I will begin the papers."

The project faltered until six years later when she began corresponding with John Greenleaf Whittier. Like his predecessor, the renowned poet at once recognized the charm of the Isles as well as Celia's potential as a writer. He offered his support: "I wish thee would write some of thy island stories and experiences, for it is too bad to waste on me alone the admirable bits of description in thy letter." (*SANDPIPER* by Rosamund Thaxter, p. 208) *"Among the Isles of Shoals"* appeared as a series of four articles in the August 1869, January, Febuary, and May 1870 issues of *The Atlantic Monthly.*

Celia's second prose commission published in *The Atlantic Monthly* detailed a horrid axe murder on Smutty-Nose Island in 1873 (*"A Memorable Murder,"* p. 269). National headlines publicizing this trial of the century immediately put the Shoals on the map, and more visitors than ever flocked to the fashionable Appledore House owned and operated by Celia's family. Train stations from Boston, Massachusetts, to Desert Isle, Maine, carried a special fifty cent travel guide edition of *Among the Isles of Shoals.*

Capitalizing on the sudden interest, The Osgood Company of Boston prepared to bring out Celia's essays in book form. Whittier, who already had played a significant role mentoring the essays, now was instrumental in soliciting his friend Harry Fenn to illustrate Celia's book of prose. In May he informs her: "I called on Mr. Anthony when in Boston. He showed me the engravings—All are good, but that of White Island is the best." Fenn's illustrations include a *Frontispiece* of White Island; Looking Southwest from Appledore; Trap Dike, Appledore; White Island (the lighthouse and cottage); and a View from the Southeastern Point of Appledore. Far more impressive than the illustrations which are in keeping with most engravings of the period, are Celia's lively descriptions of the Shoals. The writing is vivid and her exuberance for the Shoals spills out in lucid and immediate detail.

Two years later, John Scribner Jenness' THE ISLES OF SHOALS: *An Historical Sketch* fills in the chronological timeframe of the early Shoals. Although Celia does include factual information and early records in her book, she prefers an amalgamation of anecdote, legend and lore, personal observation, song and poetry. By painting an impressionistic picture of the Shoals, she accumulates texture and color much in the same way she plants her garden. Artistry, rather than conventional plotting and rigid adherence to subject matter, brings a richness of color to the reader. Thaxter's best selling AMONG THE ISLES OF SHOALS had twenty-eight printings, and has remained in print for well over a century. To the relief of Shoals enthusiasts, a recent edition conveniently indexes the material so that readers who wish to find a certain passage can return to it without paging through the entire 184-page book.

The following abridgement begins, as Celia did, with a basic description of the Shoals. It focuses on lively descriptions of pre-colonial island inhabitants, humorous old-timers' tales, and the more dramatic incidents occurring during the first two centuries of this rugged Atlantic archipelago. Constable Philip Babb of Hog Island puts in an apprearance, as do the piratical Blackbeard, buccaneers Kidd and Scott (who allegedly buried treasure on the Isles), marooned maidens, and shipwrecked sailors drowned by waves that toss island boulders around like dandelion fluff. These are but a few of the glittering treasures waiting to be discovered in this timeless creative coffer.

AMONG THE ISLES OF SHOALS

In a series of papers published not many years ago, Herman Melville made the world acquainted with the *Encantadas* or Enchanted Islands, which he describes as lying directly under the equator off the coast of South America, and of which he says: "It is to be doubted whether any spot of earth can, in desolateness, furnish a parallel to this group." But their dark volcanic crags and melancholy beaches can hardly seem more desolate than do the low bleached rocks of the Isles of Shoals to eyes that behold them for the first time.

There is a strange charm about them, an indescribable influence in their atmosphere hardly to be explained, but universally acknowledged. People forget the hurry and worry and fret of life after living there awhile.

Nine miles of the Atlantic Ocean intervene between these islands and the nearest point of the coast of New Hampshire. But from this nearest point the coastline recedes gradually, in dim and dimmer distance to Cape Ann, in Massachusetts twenty-one miles away at the southwest, and to Cape Neddock [Neddick] in Maine, sixteen miles distant in the northeast.

A word about the origin of this name, "Isles of Shoals." They are supposed to have been so called, not because the ragged reefs run out beneath the water in all directions ready to wreck and destroy, but because of the "shoaling," or "schooling" of fish about them which in the mackerel and herring seasons is remarkable. As you approach they separate and show each its own peculiar characteristics. And you perceive that there are six islands if the tide is low; but if it is high there are eight—and would be nine but that a breakwater connects two of them. Appledore, called for many years Hog Island from its rude resemblance to a hog's back rising from the water when seen from out at sea, is the largest and most regular in shape. A little valley in which are situated the buildings belonging to the house of entertainment [The Appledore House] which is the only habitation, divides its four-hundred acres into two unequal portions.

Next, almost within a stone's throw is Haley's Island, or Smutty-nose, so christened by passing sailors with a grim sense of humor, from a long black point of rock stretching out to the southeast, upon which many a ship has laid her bones. This island is low and flat and contains a greater depth of soil than the others.

At low tide, Cedar and Malaga are both connected with it—the latter permanently by a breakwater—the whole comprising about one hundred acres.

Star Island contains one hundred and fifty acres and lies a quarter of a mile southwest of Smutty-nose. Toward its northern end are clustered the houses of the little village of Gosport with a tiny church crowning the highest rock.

Not quite a mile southwest from Star, White Island lifts a lighthouse for a warning. This is the most picturesque of the group and forms, with Seavey's Island at low water, a double island with an area of some twenty acres.

Most westerly lies Londoner's, an irregular rock with a bit of beach upon which all the shells about the cluster seem to be thrown.

Two miles northeast from Appledore, Duck Island thrusts out its lurking ledges on all sides beneath the water, one of them running half a mile to the northwest. This is the most dangerous of the islands, and being the most remote, is the only one visited to any great degree by the shy sea fowl that are nearly banished by civilization.

The dividing line between Maine and New Hampshire passes through the group, giving Appledore, Smutty-nose, and Duck Islands to Maine, and the rest to New Hampshire. But their allegiance to either is a matter of small importance, the few inhabitants troubling themselves but little about what State they belong to.

The largest trap dike upon Appledore runs across the island from northeast to southwest, disappears in the sea, and reappears upon Smutty-nose, a quarter of a mile distant in a straight line. In some places, the geologist will tell you, certain deep scratches in the solid rock mean that here the glacier ground its way across the world's earlier ages. Frequently, the trap rock is honey-combed in a curious fashion—filled with small holes on the surface, as if drops of water falling for years in the same spots had worn these smooth round hollows.

Each island, every isolated rock, has its own peculiar rote, and ears made delicate by listening, in great and frequent peril, can distinguish the bearings of each in a dense fog. The threatening speech of Duck Island's ledges, the swing of the wave over Half-way Rock, the touch of the ripples on the beach at Londoner's, the long and lazy breaker that is forever rolling below the lighthouse at White Island—all are familiar and distinct, and indicate to the islander his whereabouts almost as clearly as if the sun shone brightly and no shrouding mist were striving to mock and mislead him.

Roughly rounded pebbles, not beautiful with warmth of color like those on Cohasset beaches, [south of Boston] but a cold hard combination of gray granite and dark trap, are heaped in the coves. Indian arrowheads of jasper and flint have been found among them. Now and then a smoother bit consists of a coarse gravel which, if you examine, you will find to be principally composed of shells ground fine by the waves, a fascinating mixture of blue and purple mussels lined with the rainbow tints of mother-of-pearl, and fragments of golden and ruddy snail shells, and striped and colored cockles with here and there a piece of transparent quartz (white or rosy), or of opaque feldspar faintly straw-colored, or of dull purple porphyry stone—all clean and moist with the odorous brine.

There are no trees except perhaps a few balm-of-gilead trees on Star and a small elm on Appledore which has been struggling with the bleakness of the situation some twenty years. It is very probable that the islands were wooded many years ago with spruce and pine perhaps—a rugged growth. I am certain that cedars grew there for I found on the highest part of Smutty-nose Point deep down in a crevice in the rocks a piece of a root of cedar wood which, though perfectly preserved, bore marks of great age, being worn as smooth as glass with the raindrops that had penetrated to its hiding place.

It is curious to note the varieties of plants, wildflowers, and grasses on this island alone. There are six different ferns and many delicate flowers bloom in the spring whose faces it is a continual surprise to find looking up at you from the rough ground among the rocks. Every flower seems twice as beautiful under these circumstances. And it is a fact that the salt air and a peculiar richness in the soil give a luxuriance of growth and a depth of color not found elsewhere. The pale-pink herb-Robert, for instance, blushes with a tint almost as deep as a damask rose, and as for the wild roses, I heard someone say they were as "bright as red carnations." In the spring the anemones are stained with purple and pink and yellow in a way that their sisters of the mainland seem pallid beside them. And the violets are wonderful—the blue ones so large and dark, and the delicately veined white ones rich with creamy fragrance. At Smutty-nose alone certain plants of the wicked-looking henbane (*Hyoscyamus niger*) flourish. And on Londoner's only there spreads at the top of the beach a large sea lungwort (*Mertensia maritima*). At Star the crooked little ways between the houses are lined with tall plants of the poisonous hemlock (the *Conium* that made the death-draught of Socrates) which flourishes amain and is the only green thing out of the small walled enclosures except the grass and the burdocks. For the cows and the children devastate the ground.

Appledore is altogether the most agreeable in its aspect of all the islands, being the largest and having a greater variety of surface than the rest. Its southern portion is full of interest from the traces of vanished humanity which one beholds at every step. For the ground in some places is undermined with ancient graves, and the ruined cellars of houses wherein men and women lived more than a century ago are scattered here and there to the number of seventy and more. The men and women are dust and ashes, but here are the stones they squared and laid; here are the thresholds over which so many feet have passed.

Pleasant it is to think of the brown and swarthy fisherman, the father standing on such a threshold and with the keen glance all seafaring men possess sweeping the wide horizon for signs of fair or foul weather. Or the mother, sitting in the sun on the step nursing her baby perhaps, or mending a net, or spinning. For the women here were famous spinners, and on Star Island yet are women who have not forgotten the art. Pleasanter still to think of some slender girl at twilight lingering with reluctant feet and wistful eyes that search the dusky sea for a returning sail whose glimmer is sweeter than moonlight or starlight to her sight—lingering still, though her mother calls within and the dew falls with the falling night. I love to people these solitudes again, and think that those who lived here centuries ago were decent God-fearing folk (most of them, for so tradition says) though in later years they fell into evil ways, and drank fire-water and came to grief.

It is a part of the religious belief of the Shoalers that the ruinous cairn on the summit of Appledore was built by the famous John Smith and his men when they discovered the islands in the year 1614. And I will not be so heretical as to doubt the fact, though it seems just as likely that it was set up by fishermen and sailors as a landmark. I never could be precisely certain of the site of the first meeting-house on this island, "built of brick at a very early period, possibly the first in the province," says Williamson in his *History of Maine*.

Neither is there any sign of the foundation of that "Academy" to which "even gentlemen from some of the principal towns on the sea coast sent their sons for literary instruction."

The ship Sagunto, it is said, met her destruction here as late as the year 1813 and there are faint echoes of other disasters of the kind. But the names of other ships have not come down to us. One wrecked on Appledore left only a quantity of broad silver pieces sprinkled about the rocks to tell of the calamity. A fisherman from Star paddling over in his dory to explore the coves and chasms for driftwood (for the island was uninhabited at the time) came suddenly upon the glittering coins. His amazement was boundless. After filling his pockets a sudden terror possessed him. He began to have a suspicion that something uncanny lurked at the bottom of such good fortune, (for the superstition of the natives is very great) and fled home to tell his neighbors who came in a body and made short work of the process of gathering the rest of the treasure. Occasionally, since that time, coins have been found about the southeast point whereon the unknown vessel struck and was completely destroyed.

Of course, Captain Kidd as he sailed is supposed to have made the locality one of his many hiding places. I remember being awed when a child at the story of how a certain old black Dinah, an inhabitant of Portsmouth, came out to Appledore then entirely divested of human abodes, and alone with only a divining rod for company, passed

37

several days and nights wandering over the island muttering to herself with her divining rod carefully balanced in her skinny hands. Robert Kidd's buried treasure, if it existed, never signaled from below to that mystic rod.

On Star Island, I have been told, a little three-legged black pot full of gold and silver pieces was dug up not very many years ago. And it is certainly true that Mr. Samuel Haley who lived upon and owned Smutty-nose, in building a wall turned over a large flat stone beneath which lay four bars of solid silver. He must have been a fine, energetic old fellow, that Samuel Haley. With this treasure, says tradition again, he built (at great trouble and expense) the sea wall which connects Smutty-nose with Malaga and makes a safe harbor for distressed mariners in stormy weather. Not only did Haley build the sea wall, but he erected salt works which manufactured excellent salt for the curing of fish, and stretched a ropewalk over the uneven ground to the extent of two hundred and seventy feet, and set up windmills to catch with their wide wings all the winds that blew that he might grind his own corn and wheat, and live as independently as possible of his fellow men. For that is one of the first things a settler on the Isles of Shoals finds it necessary to learn. He planted a little orchard where the soil was deepest and with much cherishing care contrived to coax his cherry trees into abundant fruitfulness.

There is much uncertainty with regard to dates and records of those old times. Mr. Haley is said to have died in 1811. But I have always heard that he was living when the Sagunto was wrecked upon his island, which happened according to the Gosport records [Star Island] in 1813. Fourteen shallow graves were quarried for the unknown dead in the iron earth, and there they lie with him who buried them a little above in the grassy slope. Here is his epitaph:

In memory of Mr. Samuel Haley
Who died in the year 1811
Aged 84
He was a man of great Ingenuity
Industry Honor and Honesty, true to his
Country & A man who did A great
Publik good in Building A
Dock & Receiving into his
Enclosure many a poor
Distressed Seaman & Fisherman
In distress of Weather.

In 1645 three brothers, Robert, John, and Richard Cutts emigrated from Wales and on their way to the continent paused at the Isles of Shoals, and finding them so pleasant, made their settlement here. Williamson mentions particularly

Richard Gibson from Topsham, England, and various other
men from England and Wales. Many people speedily joined
the little colony which grew yearly more prosperous. In
1650 the Rev. John Brock came to live among the islanders
and remained with them twelve years.

Last summer I was shown a quaint little book entitled
*The Fisherman's Calling: A Brief Essay To Serve The Great
Interests Of Religion Among Our Fishermen* by Cotton
Mather, D.D., Boston in New England, printed-sold by T.
Green, 1712. And I found the following incident connected
with Mr. Brock's ministry at the Shoals:

> When our Mr. Brock lived on the Isles of Shoals, he brought
> the Fishermen into an agreement that besides the Lord's Day
> they would spend one day of every month together in the
> worship of the Glorious Lord. A certain day which by their
> Agreement belonged unto the Exercises of Religion being
> arrived, they came to Mr. Brock and asked him that they
> might put by their meeting and go a Fishing, because they had
> Lost many Days by the Foulness of the weather. He, seeing
> that without and against his consent they resolved upon doing
> what they asked of him, replied: 'If you will go away I say
> unto you, Catch Fish if you can! But as for you that will tarry
> and worship our Lord Jesus Christ this day, I will pray unto
> Him for you that you may afterwards take fish till you are
> weary.' Thirty men went away from the meeting and Five
> tarried. The thirty that went away from the meeting with all

their Craft could catch but four Fishes. The Five which tarried went forth afterwards and they took Five Hundred! The Fishermen were after this Readier to hearken unto the Voice of their Teacher.

Philip Babb of Hog Island [Appledore] was appointed constable for all the islands of Shoals [Star Island excepted]. There were then about forty families on Hog Island. But between that time [1652] and the year 1670 these removed to Star Island and joined the settlement there. This they were induced to do partly through fear of the Indians who frequented Duck Island and thence made plundering excursions upon them, carrying off their women while they were absent fishing, and doing a variety of harm. But, as it is expressly stated that people living on the mainland sent their children to school at Appledore that they might be safe from the Indians, the statement of their depredations at the Shoals is perplexing. Probably the savages camped on Duck to carry on their craft of porpoise fishing, which to this day they still pursue among the islands on the eastern coast of Maine. Star Island seemed a place of greater safety, and probably the greater advantages of landing and the convenience of a wide cove at the entrance of the village with a little harbor wherein the fishing craft might anchor with some security were also inducements.

From three to four thousand quintals of fish were yearly caught and cured by the islanders, and beside their trade with Spain, large quantities of fish were also carried to Portsmouth for the West India market.

Tucke was the only one who closed his life and ministry at the Shoals. He was a graduate of Harvard College of the class of 1723, was ordained at the Shoals July 20, 1732, and died there August 12, 1773—his ministry thus covering more than forty years. His salary in 1771 was paid in merchantable fish, a quintal to a man, when there were on the Shoals from ninety to one hundred men and a quintal of fish was worth a guinea. At the time of Mr. Tucke's death the prosperity of the Shoals was at its height. But in less than thirty years after his death a most woeful condition of things was inaugurated.

The settlement flourished till the breaking out of the war [the American Revolution] when it was found to be entirely at the mercy of the English, and obliged to furnish them with recruits and supplies. The inhabitants were therefore ordered by the government to quit the islands. Those who remained, with a few exceptions, were among the most ignorant and degraded of the people, and they went rapidly down into untold depths of misery. In no place of the size has there been a greater absorption of rum since the world was made.

The old town records are quaint and interesting, and the spelling and modes of expression so peculiar that I have copied a few:

This is a Leagel vot by the ton meeting, that if any presson or pressons shall leave their Cowks out after the fifteenth day of May and they do any Dameg, they shall be taken up and the owner of the kow shall pay teen shillings old tenor to the kow constabel and one half he shall have and the other shall give to the pour of the place.

MR DANIEL RANDEL

"Kow Constabel."

Among the offorsers of Gospored were, besides Moderator and Town Clarke, Seelekt meen, Counstauble, Tidon meen (Tithing men) Coulears of fish (Coulear meaning, I suppose, culler or person appointed to select fish), and Sealers of Whood, (oftener expressed Corders of Wood).

It would seem strange that while they live in so healthy a place where the atmosphere is absolutely perfect in its purity, they should have suffered so much from ill health. I have seen a little room containing a whole family, fishing boots and all, bed, furniture, cooking stove in full blast, and an oil lamp with a wick so high that the deadly smoke rose steadily, filling the air with what Browning might call "filthiest gloom," and mingling with the incense of ancient tobacco pipes smoked by both sexes. (For nearly all the old women used to smoke.) Every crack and cranny was stopped and if, by any chance the door opened for an instant, out rushed a fume in comparison with which the gusts from the lake of Tartarus might be imagined sweet. Shut in that deadly air, a part of the family slept—sometimes all. What wonder that their chests were hollow, their faces haggard, and that apathy settled upon them! Then their food was hardly selected with reference to health, saleratus [sodium bicarbonate] and pork forming two of the principal ingredients in their daily fare.

But there are sensible fellows among them, fine specimens of the hardy New England fisherman. Nothing can be more satisfactory than the blendings and contrasts of color and the picturesque effect of the general aspect of the natives in their element. The eye is often struck with the richness of the color of some rough hand, glowing with mingled red, brown, and orange, against the gray-blue water, as it grasps an oar, perhaps, or pulls in a rope. It is strange that the sun and wind, which give such fine tints to the complexions of the lords of creation, should leave such hideous traces on the faces of women. When they are exposed to the same salt wind and clear sunshine, they take the hue of dried fish, and become objects for men and angels to weep over.

Anxious lives they have led, especially the women, many of whom have grown old before their time with hard work and bitter cares, with hewing of wood and drawing of water, turning of fish on the flakes to dry in the sun, endless household work, and the cares of maternity—while their lords lounged about the rocks in their scarlet shirts in the sun or "held up the walls of the meeting-house," as one expressed it, with their brawny shoulders. I never saw such wrecks of humanity as some of the old women on Star Island who have long since gone to their rest. In my childhood I caught glimpses of them occasionally, their lean brown shapes crouching over the fire with black pipes in their sunken mouths and hollow eyes of no use now but to gather brine, and rough, gray, straggling locks. Despoiled and hopeless visions, it seemed as if youth and joy could never have been theirs.

The local pronunciation of the Shoalers is very peculiar, and a shrewd sense of humor is one of their leading characteristics. Their sense of fun showed itself in the nicknames with which they designated any person possessing the slightest peculiarity. For instance, twenty years ago a minister of the Methodist persuasion came to live among them. His wife was unreasonably tall and thin. With the utmost promptitude and decision, the irreverent christened her "Legs," and never spoke of her by any other name. "Laigs has gone to Portsmouth," or "Laigs has got a new gown." A spinster of very dark complexion was called "Scip," an abbreviation of Scipio, a name supposed to appertain particularly to the colored race. Another was called "Squint," because of a defect in the power of vision. And not only were they spoken of by these names, but called so to their faces habitually. One man earned for himself the title of "Brag," so that no one ever thought of calling him by his real name. His wife was Mrs. Brag, and constant use so robbed these names of their offensiveness that the bearers not only heard them with equanimity, but would hardly have known themselves by their true ones. A most worthy Norwegian took up his abode for a brief space among them a few years ago. His name was Ingebertsen. Now, to expect any Shoaler would trouble himself to utter such a name as that was beyond all reason. At once they called him "Carpenter," (apropos of nothing at all for he never had been a carpenter). But the name was the first that occurred to them, and sufficiently easy of utterance. It was "Carpenter," and "Mis' Carpenter," and "them Carpenter children," and the name still clings to fine old Ingebertsen and his family. Grandparents are addressed as Grans and Gwammaye, (Grans being an abbreviation of Grandsire).

In pleasant weather sometimes the younger women would paddle from one island to another making calls. If any old Grans perceived them loafing at his door in the sun, "It's going to storm. The women begin to flit!" he would cry as if they were a flock of coots. Two boys in bitter contention have been heard calling each other "nasty-faced chowder-heads," as if the force of language could no further go. "I'm dryer than a graven image," a man says when he is thirsty.

But it is impossible to give an idea of their common speech leaving out the profanity which makes it so startling.

Nearly all the Shoalers have a singular gait contracted from the effort to keep their equilibrium while standing in boats, and from the unavoidable gymnastics which any attempt at locomotion among the rocks renders necessary. Some stiff-jointed old men have been known to leap wildly from broad stone to stone on the smooth, flat pavements of Portsmouth town, finding it out of the question to walk evenly and decorously along the straight and easy way.

They all seemed to think it necessary to shut their eyes and squirm like nothing human during the process of singing a song, and they pitched the tune so high that no human voice ever could hope to reach it in safety. "Tew high, Bill. Tew high," one would say to the singer with slow solemnity. So Bill tried again. "Tew high again, Bill. Tew high." "Wull, *you* strike it, Obed," Bill would say in despair. And Obed would strike and hit exactly the same impossible altitude, whereat Bill would slap his knee and cry in glad surprise, "D—d if he ain't got it!" and forthwith catch Obed and launch on his perilous flight and grow red in the face with the mighty effort of getting up there and remaining there through the intricacies and variations of the melody. One could but wonder whence these queer tunes came— how they were created? Some of them reminded one of the creaking and groaning of windlasses and masts, the rattling of rowlocks, the whistling of winds among cordage—yet with less music in them than these natural sounds.

The process of dunning which made the Shoals fish so famous a century ago is almost a lost art. A real dunfish is handsome, cut in transparent strips the color of brown sherry wine. The process is a tedious one. The fish are piled in the storehouse and undergo a period of "sweating" after the first drying, then are carried out into sun and wind, dried again slightly, and again piled in the warehouse and so on till the process is complete. Drying fish in the common fashion is more difficult than might be imagined. It is necessary to watch and tend them continually as they lie on the picturesque "flakes." And if they are exposed at too early a stage to a sun too hot they burn as surely as a loaf of bread in an intemperate oven. Only, the burning does not crisp, but liquefies their substance.

The process of drawing [in] the trawl is very picturesque and interesting watched from the rocks or from the boat itself. The buoy being drawn in, then follow the baited hooks one after another. First, perhaps, a rockling shows his bright head above water. A pull, and in he comes, flapping with brilliant red fins, distended gaping mouth, indigo-colored eyes, and richly mottled skin. A few futile somersets and he subsides into slimy dejection. Next, perhaps a big whelk is tossed into the boat. Then a leaden-gray haddock with its dark stripe of color on each side.

Then, perhaps follow a few bare hooks. Then a hake with horrid cavernous mouth. Then a large purple star fish or a clattering crab. Then a ling—a yellow-brown, wide-mouthed piece of ugliness never eaten here but highly esteemed on the coast of Scotland. Then more cod or haddock, or perhaps a lobster bristling with indignation at the novel situation in which he finds himself. Then a cusk, long, smooth, compact and dark. Then a catfish.

Of all fiends, commend me to the catfish as the most fiendish! Black as night with thick and hideous skin which looks a dull moldy green beneath the water, a head shaped as much like a cat's as a fish's head can be, in which the devil's own eyes seem to glow with a dull malicious gleam. And such a mouth! What terrible expressions these cold creatures carry to and fro in the vast, dim spaces of the sea. All fish have a more or less imbecile and woebegone aspect. But this one looks absolutely evil. And Schiller might well say of him that he "grins through the grate of his spiky teeth," and sharp and deadly are they. Every man looks out for his boots when a catfish comes tumbling in, for they bite through leather, flesh, and bones. They seize a ballast stone between their jaws and their teeth snap and fly in all directions. I have seen them bite the long blade of a sharp knife so fiercely that when it was lifted and held aloft, they kept their furious grip and dangled, flapping all their clumsy weight, hanging by their teeth to the blade.

49

Wolf-fish (first cousins to the catfish) are found also on the trawls. And dog-fish with pointed snouts and sandpaper skins abound to such an extent as to drive away everything else sometimes. Sand-dabs, a kind of flounder, fasten their sluggish bodies to the hooks. And a few beautiful red fish called bream are occasionally found. Also a few blue fish and sharks. Frequently halibut, though these latter are generally caught on trawls which are made especially for them. Sometimes is caught on a trawl a monstrous creature of horrible aspect called the nurse-fish—an immense fish weighing twelve hundred pounds, with a skin like a nutmeg grater and no teeth, a kind of sucker (hence its name). I asked a Shoaler what the nurse-fish looked like and he answered promptly, "Like the Devil!"

One of the fishermen described a creature which they call mud eel, a foot and a half long with a mouth like a rat and two teeth. The bite of this water snake is poisonous— the islanders aver, and tell a story of a man bitten by one at Mount Desert last year who did not live long enough to get to the doctor. They bite at the hooks on the trawl and are drawn up in a lump of mud, and the men cut the ropes and mangle their lines to get rid of them.

Swordfish also are harpooned, weighing eight hundred pounds and upward. They are very delicate food. It is a lovely sight to see a herring net drawn in, especially by moonlight when every fish hangs like a long silver drop from the close-set meshes. Perch are found in inexhaustible quantities about the rocks, and lump or butter fish are sometimes caught. Pollock are very plentiful—smooth, graceful, slender creatures.

Whales are more or less plentiful in summer spouting their foam fountains in the sea. Beautiful is the sparkling column of water rising suddenly afar off and falling noiselessly back again. Not long ago a whale twisted his tail in the cable of the schooner Vesper lying to the eastward of the Shoals, and towed the vessel several miles at the rate of twenty knots an hour with the water boiling all over her from stem to stern.

Last winter some of the Shoalers were drawing a trawl between the Shoals and Boone Island fifteen miles to the eastward. As they drew in the line and relieved each hook of its burden, lo a horror was lifted half above the surface—part of a human body which dropped off the hooks and was gone while they shuddered and stared at each other.

If summer is a laggard in her coming, she makes up for it by the loveliness of her lingering into autumn. Then there are mornings when all in the blue unclouded weather the coast line comes out so distinctly that houses, trees, bits of white beach, are clearly visible. And with a glass, moving forms of carriages and cattle are distinguishable nine miles away. In the transparent air the peaks of Mounts

Madison, Washington, and Jefferson are seen distinctly at a distance of one hundred miles. Poets are not wrong who talk of purple seas. The air is clear and sparkling. The lovely summer haze withdraws. All things take a crisp and tender outline, and the cry of the curlew and the plover is doubly sweet through the pure cool air. Then sunsets burn in clear and tranquil skies or flame in piled magnificence of clouds.

At the first biting cold, the distant mainland has the appearance of being taken off its feet as it were—the line distorted, detached from the water at both ends; it is as if one looked under it and saw the sky beyond. Then, on bright mornings with a brisk wind, little wafts of mist rise between the quick short waves and melt away before noon. At some periods of intense cold these mists, which are never in banks like fog, rise in irregular whirling columns reaching to the clouds—shadowy phantoms, torn and wild, that stalk past like Ossian's ghosts solemnly and noiselessly throughout the bitter day. When the sun drops down behind these weird processions with a dark-red lurid light, it is like a vast conflagration wonderful and terrible to see. The columns that strike and fall athwart the island sweep against the windows with a sound like sand and lie on the ground in ridges like fine sharp hail. Yet the heavens are clear, the heavily rolling sea dark-green and white, and between the breaking crests the misty columns stream toward the sky.

In December the colors seem to fade out of the world and utter ungraciousness prevails. Each island wears its chalk-white girdle of ice between the rising and falling tides (edged with black at low water, where the lowest growing seaweed is exposed), making the stern bare rocks above more forbidding by their contrast with its stark whiteness. And the whiteness of salt-water ice is ghastly.

The weather becomes of the first importance to the dwellers on the rock. The changes of the sky and sea, the flitting of the coasters to and fro, the visits of the sea fowl, sunrise and sunset, the changing moon, the northern lights, the constellations that wheel in splendor through the winter night—all are noted with a love and careful scrutiny that is seldom given by people living in populous places. One grows accustomed to the aspect of the constellations and they seem like the faces of old friends looking down out of the awful blackness. And when in summer the great Orion disappears, how it is missed out of the sky!

The best balanced human mind is prone to lose its elasticity and stagnate in this isolation. And in this matter women have the advantage of men who are condemned to fold their hands when their tasks are done. . . With a bright and cheerful interior, open fires, books and pictures, windows full of thrifty blossoming plants and climbing vines, a family of singing birds, plenty of work, and a clear head and quiet conscience, it would go hard if one could not be happy— even in such loneliness.

The few schooners moored about the islands become so loaded with ice that sometimes they sink. Every plunge into the assailing waves adds a fresh crust, infinitely thin. But in twenty-four hours enough accumulates to sink the vessel. And it is part of the day's work in the coldest weather to beat off the ice—and hard work it is. Every time the bowsprit dips under, the man who sits astride it is immersed to his waist in the freezing water as he beats at the bow to free the laboring craft. I cannot imagine a harder life than the sailors lead in winter in the coasting vessels that stream in endless processions to and fro along the shore. And they seem to be the hardest set of people under the sun—so rough and reckless that they are not pleasant even at a distance.

Sometimes they land here. A crew of thirteen or fourteen came on shore last winter. They might have been the ghosts of the men who manned the picaroons that used to swarm in these seas. A more piratical looking set could not well be imagined. They roamed about and glared in at the windows with weather-beaten, brutal faces, and eyes that showed traces of whiskey, ugly and unmistakable.

I never shall forget one long dreary, drizzly northeast storm when two men rowed across from Star to Appledore on this errand; a little child had died, and they could not sail to the mainland and had no means to construct a coffin among themselves. All day I watched the making of that little chrysalis. And at night the last nail was driven in and it lay across a bench in the midst of the litter of the workshop and a curious stillness seemed to emanate from the senseless boards. I went back to the house and gathered a handful of scarlet geranium and returned with it through the rain. The brilliant blossoms were sprinkled with glittering drops. I laid them in the little coffin while the wind wailed so sorrowfully outside and the rain poured against the windows. Two men came through the mist and storm, and one swung the light little shell to his shoulder and they carried it away and the gathering darkness shut down and hid them as they tossed among the waves.

A calm preceded the storm which destroyed the Minot's Ledge Lighthouse in 1849. I never knew such silence. Though the sun blazed without a cloud, the sky and sea were utterly wan and colorless, and before sunset the mysterious tone began to vibrate in the breezeless air. "Hog Island's crying!" said the islanders. One could but think of the *Ancient Mariner* as the angry sun went down in a brassy glare. And still no ripple broke the calm. But with the twilight gathered the waiting wind, slowly and steadily. And before morning the shock of the breakers was like the incessant thundering of heavy guns. The solid rock perceptibly trembled. Windows shook and glass and china rattled in the house.

It is impossible to describe the confusion, the tumult, the rush and roar and thunder of waves and wind overwhelming those rocks—the whole Atlantic rushing headlong to cast itself upon them. It was very exciting. The most timid among us lost all sense of fear. Before the next night the sea had made a breach through the valley on Appledore in which the houses stand—a thing that never had happened within the memory of the oldest inhabitant. The waves piled in from the eastward (where Old Harry was tossing the breakers sky-high)—a maddened troop of giants sweeping every-thing before them, and flowed one another white as milk through the valley from east to west, strewing the space with boulders from a solid wall six feet high and as many thick which ran across the top of the beach [the breakwater] and which one tremendous wave toppled over like a child's fence of blocks. Kelp and seaweed were piled in banks high up along the shore and strewed the doorsteps. And thou-sands of the hideous creatures known among the Shoalers as sea-mice, (a *holothurian*-livid, shapeless mass of torpid life) were scattered in all directions.

While the storm was at its height it was impossible to do anything but watch it through windows beaten by the blinding spray which burst in flying clouds all over the island, drenching every inch of the soil in foaming brine.

In the coves the yeasty surges were churned into yellow masses of foam that blew across in trembling flakes and clung wherever they lit, leaving a hoary scum of salt when dry, which remained till sweet fair water dropped out of the clouds to wash it all away. It was long before the sea went down and days after the sun began to shine. The fringe of spray still leaped skyward from the eastern shore, and Shag and Mingo Rocks at Duck Island tossed their distant clouds of snow against the blue.

The sea broke the windows of the house several times during our stay at the lighthouse. [Celia was a child.] Everything shook so violently from the concussion of the breakers that dishes on the closet shelves fell to the floor. One night when, from the southeast, the very soul of chaos seemed to have been let loose upon the world, the whole ponderous walk [the covered bridge that connected the house and lighthouse] was carried thundering down the gorge and dragged out into the raging sea.

Once or twice every year came the black, lumbering old oil schooner that brought supplies for the lighthouse and the inspector who gravely examined everything to see if all was in order. He left stacks of clear red and white glass chimneys for the lamps, and several doe-skins for polishing the great silver-lined copier reflectors, large bundles of wicks, and various pairs of scissors for trimming them, heavy black casks of ill-perfumed whale-oil, and other things which were all stowed in the round, dimly lighted rooms of the tower. Very awe-struck, we children always crept into corners and whispered and watched the intruders till they embarked in their ancient clumsy vessel, and, hoisting their dark weather-stained sails, bore slowly away again. About ten years ago that old white lighthouse was taken away and a new perpendicular brick tower built in its place. The lantern with its fifteen lamps, ten golden and five red, gave place to Fresnel's powerful single burner (or rather, three burners in one) enclosed in its case of prisms. The old lighthouse was by far the most picturesque. But perhaps the new one is more effective, the light being undoubtedly more powerful.

We hardly saw a human face beside our own all winter. But with the spring came manifold life to our lonely dwelling—human life among other forms. Our neighbors from Star rowed across. The pilot boat from Portsmouth steered over and brought us letters, newspapers, magazines, and told us the news of months. The faint echoes from the far-off world hardly touched us little ones. We listened to the talk of our elders: Winfield Scott and Santa Anna, the war in Mexico, the famine in Ireland. It all meant nothing to us. We heard the reading aloud of details of famine and saw tears in the eyes of the reader and were vaguely sorry. But the fate of Red Riding-Hood was much more near and dreadful to us.

I had a scrap of garden literally not more than a yard square wherein grew only African marigolds, rich in color as barbaric gold. I knew nothing of John Keats at that time. But I am sure he never felt their beauty more devoutly than the little half-savage being who knelt like a fire worshipper to watch the unfolding of those golden disks. When later the brave new world of poets was opened to me, with what power those glowing lines of his went straight to my heart: "Open afresh your rounds of starry folds, ye ardent marigolds!"

Unafraid, too, we watched the summer tempests. And here I am reminded of a story told by some gentlemen visiting Appledore sixteen or eighteen years ago. They started from Portsmouth for the Shoals in a whale-boat one evening in summer with a native Star Islander, Richard Randall by name, to manage the boat. They had sailed about half the distance when they were surprised at seeing a large ball of fire like a rising moon rolling toward them over the sea from the south. They watched it eagerly as it bore down upon them and, veering off, went east of them at some little distance and then passed astern. And there, of course, they expected to lose sight of it, but while they were marveling and speculating, it altered its course and suddenly began to near them, coming back upon its track against the wind and steadily following in their wake. This was too much for the native Shoaler. He took off his jacket and turned it inside out to exorcise the fiend. And lo, the

apparition most certainly disappeared! It was never satisfactorily accounted for and must remain a mystery.

It has been my good fortune to witness but few wrecks
at the Shoals. A resident at Star Island told me of a wreck
which took place forty-seven years ago. It blew so that all
the doors in the house opened as fast as they shut them, and
in the night a vessel drove against Hog Island Head which
fronts the village [Gosport] on Star. She went to pieces
utterly. In the morning the islanders perceived the beach at
Londoners heaped with some kind of drift. They could not
make out what it was, but as soon as the sea subsided went
to examine, and found a mass of oranges and picture frames
with which the vessel had been freighted. Not a soul was
saved. She struck with such force that she drove a large
spike out of her forefoot into a crevice in the rock, which
was plainly to be seen till a few years ago. My informant
also told me that she remembered the wreck of the Sagunto
in 1813—that the beaches were strewn with almond nuts
long after, and that she picked up curiously embroidered
vests and work-bags in all directions along the shores.

In later years a few coasters and fishermen have gone
ashore at the islands, generally upon the hidden ledges at
Duck. Many of these have been loaded with lime—a most
perilous freight, for as soon as the water touches it there is
a double danger, and between fire and water there is little
chance of escape.

One of the most hideous experiences I have heard befell a young Norwegian now living at the Shoals. He and a young companion came out from Portsmouth to set their trawl in the winter fishing two years ago. Before they reached the island came a sudden squall of wind and snow, chilling and blinding. In a few moments they knew not where they were, and the wind continued to sweep them away. The keepers at the lighthouse saw the poor fellows but were powerless to help them. Alas the road-lines soon broke, and the little boat was swept off again, they knew not whither. Night came down upon them, tossed on that terrible black sea. The snow ceased, the clouds flew before the deadly cold northwest wind, the thermometer sank below zero. One of the men died before morning. The other, alone with the dead man, was still driven on and on before the pitiless gale. Before night he passed Cape Cod and knew it as he rushed by. Another unspeakably awful night and the gale abated no whit. Next morning he was almost gone from cold, fatigue and hunger. His eyes were so swollen he could hardly see. But afar off, shining whiter than silver in the sun, the sails of a large schooner appeared at the edge of the fearful wilderness. He managed to hoist a bit of old canvas on an oar. He was then not far from Holmes' Hole nearly two hundred miles from the Shoals!

The schooner saw it and bore down for him, but the sea was running so high that he expected to be swamped every instant. As she swept past they threw from the deck a rope with a loop at the end tied with a bow-line knot that would not slip. It caught him over the head, and clutching it at his throat with both hands, in an instant he found himself in the sea among the ice-cold furious waves, drawn toward the vessel with all the strength of her crew. Just before he emerged he heard the captain shout, "We've lost him!" Ah the bitter moment, for a horrible fear struck through him that they might lose their hold an instant on the rope, and then he knew it would be all over. But they saved him. The boat with the dead man in it all alone went tossing heaven knows where.

There is a superstition among the islanders that Philip Babb [settled on Hog Island, 1652, died 1671] or some evil-minded descendant of his still haunts Appledore, and no consideration would induce the more timid to walk alone after dark over a certain shingly beach on that island at the top of a cove bearing Babb's name—for there the uneasy spirit is oftenest seen. One of the Shoalers is perfectly certain that he and Babb have met, and he shudders with real horror recalling the meeting.

This is his story: It was after sunset (of course) and he was coming round the corner of a workshop when he saw a wild and dreadful figure advancing toward him. His first thought was that someone wished to make him the victim of a practical joke. And he called out something to the effect that he wasn't afraid. But the thing came near with ghastly face and hollow eyes, and assuming a fiendish expression, took out the knife from its belt [he is thought to have been a butcher] and flourished it in the face of the Shoaler who fled to the house and entered breathless, calling for the person whom he supposed had tried to frighten him. That person was quietly eating his supper, and when the poor fellow saw him he was so much agitated that he nearly fainted.

The whole Babb family are buried in the valley of Appledore where the houses stand, and till this year a bowling alley stood upon the spot and all the balls rolled over the bones of all the Babbs. That may have been one reason why the head of the family was so restless. Since the last equinoctial gale blew the building down, perhaps he may rest more peacefully.

There is a superstition here and along the coast to this effect: a man gathering driftwood or whatever it may be sees a spade stuck in the ground as if inviting him to dig. He isn't quite ready, goes and empties his basket first, then comes back to investigate, and lo there's nothing there. And he is tormented the rest of his life with the thought that probably untold wealth lay beneath that spade which he might have possessed had he only been wise enough to seize the treasure when it offered itself. A certain man named William Mace [a settler of Babb's time] living at Star long, long ago swore that he had had this experience. And there's a dim tradition that another person, seeing the spade, passed by about his business, but hastening back, arrived just in time to see the last of the sinking tool and to perceive also a golden flat-iron disappearing into the earth. This he seized. But no human power could extricate it from the ground, and he was forced to let go his hold and see it sink out of his longing ken.

I have before me a weird romantic legend of these islands in a time-stained, battered newspaper of forty years ago. The unknown writer tells his story well. He came to the Shoals for the benefit of his failing health and remained there late into the autumn of 1826 in the family of a worthy fisherman.

He tells his strange story in this way: It was one of those awfully still mornings which cloud gazers will remember as characterizing the autumn months. There was not a single vapor-wreath to dim the intense blue of the sky, or a breath to ruffle the almost motionless repose of the great deep. Even the sunlight fell seemingly with stiller brightness on the surface of it. He stood on a low long point fronting the east with the cliffs behind him gazing out upon the calm when suddenly he became aware of a figure standing near him. It was a woman wrapped closely in a dark sea cloak with a profusion of light hair flowing loosely over her shoulders. Fair as a lily and as still, she stood with her eyes fixed on the far distance without a motion, without a sound. Thinking her one of the inhabitants of a neighboring island who was watching for the return of a fishing boat or perhaps a lover, he did not immediately address her. But seeing no appearance of any vessel, at length accosted her with, "Well, my pretty maiden, do you see anything of him?" She turned instantly and fixing on him the largest and most melancholy blue eyes ever beheld, said quietly, "He *will* come again." Fairly at home again, he was inclined to look upon his adventure as a dream, a mere delusion arising from his illness, but concluded to seek in his surroundings something to substantiate or remove the idea. Finding nothing—no woman on the island resembling the one he had met—and hearing of no circumstance which might corroborate the unaccountable impression, he resolved to go again to the same spot. This time it blew half a gale. The fishermen in vain endeavored to dissuade him. He was so intensely anxious to be assured of the truth or fiction of the impression of the day before that he could not refrain and launched his boat which sprang strongly upon the whitened waters. And unfurling his one sail, he rounded a point and was soon safely sheltered in a small cove on the leeward side of the island, probably Babb's Cove.

Then he leaped the chasms and made his way to the scene of his bewilderment. The sea was rolling over the low point—the spot where he had stood the day before was a chaos of tumult, yet even then he could have sworn that he heard with the same deep distinctness the quiet words of the maiden, "He *will* come again," and then a low remotely ringing laughter.

So sweet a ghost was hardly a salutary influence in the life of our invalid. She held him with her glittering eye till he grew quite beside himself. This is so good a description I cannot choose but quote it: "The last time I stood with her was just at the evening of a tranquil day. It was a lovely sunset. A few gold-edged clouds crowned the hills of the distant continent, and the sun had gone down behind them. Kneeling in shuddering fearfulness I swore never more to look upon that spot, and never did again."

At the time of the first settlement, the islands were infested by pirates—the bold Captain Teach, called Blackbeard, being one of the most notorious. One of Teach's comrades, a Captain Scot, brought this lovely lady hither. They buried immense treasure on the islands. That of Scot was buried on an island apart from the rest. Before they departed on a voyage to plunder, slash and slay (in which, by the way, they were involved in one awful doom by the blowing up of a powder magazine), the maiden was carried to the island where her pirate lover's treasure was hidden and made to swear with horrible rites that until his return (if it were not till the day of judgement) she would guard it from the search of all mortals. So there she paces still.

POEMS

Preface

Celia Thaxter started writing poems while she was a mother of three sons, mistress of a large house in Newtonville, Massachusetts, and wife to an unemployed husband. These first verses look back at her carefree childhood on the Isles of Shoals and convey her longing for the sea.

One humdrum day in March 1860 Celia picked up a copy of *The Atlantic Monthly* literary magazine and was surprised to discover one of her poems, "Land-locked," staring out at her in bold print. She had read the poem to Karl who, though the oldest, lagged far behind his brothers in reading skills. She also had written out copies for her husband Levi, her friend Lizzie Curzon, and her brothers. All of them flatly denied having submitted the poem to the magazine.

Encouraged by the praise for her first publication, Celia's spirits lifted, and soon between household chores she was writing and submitting poems to the new magazine editor, James Fields.

Levi also was making a name for himself by championing the poetry of Robert Browning. His dramatic readings of the British poet's work won him a coveted entree into the prestigious Saturday Club (men only) of Boston. Celia's poems and her romantic island background plus Levi's contacts with Henry Wadsworth Longfellow,

Thomas Wentworth Higginson, Oliver Wendell Holmes, Harriet Beecher Stowe and other literary luminaries worked like a charm. Before long, the young couple were at the very center of Boston's literary circle, and highly in demand. Celebrated poet John Greenleaf Whitter solicited poems and stories from Celia for a children's magazine, and soon commissions and submissions were paying the household bills.

In 1871 Levi Thaxter plunked down $500 to publish his wife's first collection of poetry. The book elicited glowing reviews, and in 1874 and 1876 Houghton, Osgood & Co. reprinted the collection. From then on, Celia brought out new poems every two or three years. The volumes include *Drift-Weed* (1879), *Poems For Children* (1883), *The Cruise Of The Mystery And Other Poems* (1886) and two commercial booklets, *Yule Log* (1889) and *My Lighthouse* (1891) illustrated and distributed by the Prang Watercolor Company.

In the preface to the posthumous Appledore Edition of Thaxter's collected poems, her friend and colleague Sarah Orne Jewett observes: "The poems seem to make something like a journal of her daily life and thought." Readers will discover this inextricable link between Celia's life and her poetry in the following selection taken from two major works: *THE POEMS OF CELIA THAXTER* (Appledore Edition, Houghton Mifflin, 1896, 266 pp) and STORIES AND POEMS

70

FOR CHILDREN, (Houghton Mifflin, 1895, pp 113-257). Characteristic of the era, the posthumous Appledore Edition masses collections together without any indication where one ends and the other begins. *The Cruise Of The Mystery* has been tacked on at page 177, and eleven unpublished poems after that.

Victorian printers notoriously made a mess of poetic form, breaking up longer lines at the least likely spot because they wouldn't fit the page. What the poet intended as a four line stanza often might end up with three or four tag lines or widows (isolated one-word lines). Like other authors of the day, Celia submitted her original manuscript in longhand and was at the mercy of these haphazard printing oversights. Here, obvious word, line, and stanza gaffs have been edited out and the poems are clearly formatted in a reasonable sequence for today's reader.

In the introduction to a reprint of Celia Thaxter's prose, one contemporary editor discourages readers from searching out her poetry. Poets like Celia "who speak to and for the people of their own day often have little to say a century later," he writes.

True, the Os and Ahs, Thees and Thys do take us back to an era of piazzas and parasols. Yet anyone who has visited the Shoals will immediately identify and appreciate the eternal seascape Celia portrays with such a natural, unassuming gift. "Something strangely full and bright came to her verse from that mystical environment of the ocean," comments reviewer William Dean Howells.

The lilt of the ocean buoys up the poems as well as Celia's ear for music. We're told she had a pleasant singing voice and played the aeolian harp. Her COLLECTED VERSE includes no less than fourteen "Songs." She also had an excellent reading voice and, Annie Fields writes, "summer after summer listeners would gather if she would promise to read to them."

Contemporary critics who summarily dismiss Thaxter's poetry as dated surely haven't read the poems Starlight, The Great Blue Heron: A Warning, or Minute Guns. With consummate skill, this independent, forward-looking woman rhapsodizes about outer space, vilifies the killing of birds, and writes war protest poems. In the next breath she is penning a lullaby for her newborn son and songs for a lover. The poems demonstrate a remarkable craft with a variety of forms and subject matter from ballads about shipwrecks and verses in dialogue to love sonnets and odes extolling poppy seeds and ferns.

Thaxter's complete poems comprise a valuable record not only of the nature and history of a place but of an extraordinary literary era. Perhaps someday they will be annotated, indexed, and on the shelf alongside Emily Dickinson's collected work—Emily, The Belle of Amherst who never saw the sea—and Celia, The Island Queen, who always saw it.

CONTENTS

OVER THE LIGHTHOUSE

THE SANDPIPER

Across the narrow beach we flit,
  one little sandpiper and I,
and fast I gather, bit by bit,
  the scattered driftwood bleached and dry;
the wild waves reach their hands for it.
  The wild wind raves, the tide runs high
as up and down the beach we flit—
  one little sandpiper and I.

Above our heads the sullen clouds
  scud black and swift across the sky;
like silent ghosts in misty shrouds
  stand out the white lighthouses high.
Almost as far as eye can reach
  I see the close-reefed vessels fly
as fast we flit along the beach—
  one little sandpiper and I.

I watch him as he skims along
   uttering his sweet and mournful cry.
He starts not at my fitful song
   or flash of fluttering drapery.
He has no thought of any wrong;
   he scans me with a fearless eye.
Staunch friends are we, well tried and strong,
   the little sandpiper and I.

Comrade, where wilt thou be tonight
   when the loosed storm breaks furiously?
My driftwood fire will burn so bright!
   To what warm shelter canst thou fly?
I do not fear for thee, though wroth
   the tempest rushes through the sky;
for are we not God's children both,
   thou, little sandpiper, and I?

THE SHAG

"What is that great bird, Sister, tell me,
  perched high on the top of the crag?"
"Tis the cormorant, dear little Brother.
  The fishermen call it the shag."

"But what does it there, Sister, tell me,
  sitting lonely against the black sky?"
"It has settled to rest, little Brother.
  It hears the wild gale wailing high."

"But I am afraid of it, Sister,
  for over the sea and the land
  it gazes, so black and so silent!"
"Little Brother, hold fast to my hand."

"Oh, what was that, Sister, the thunder?
  Did the shag bring the storm and the cloud,
  the wind and the rain and the lightning?"
"Little Brother, the thunder roars loud—

Run fast, for the rain sweeps the ocean.
Look! Over the lighthouse it streams.
And the lightning leaps red, and above us
the gulls fill the air with their screams."

O'er the beach, o'er the rocks, running swiftly,
the little white cottage they gain;
and safely they watch from the window
the dance and the rush of the rain.

But the shag kept his place on the headland,
and when the brief storm had gone by,
he shook his loose plumes, and they saw him
rise splendid and strong in the sky.

Clinging fast to the gown of his sister,
the little boy laughed as he flew:
"He is gone with the wind and the lightning,
and I am not frightened—are you?"

THE WATER BLOOM

A child looked up in the summer sky
where a soft bright shower had just passed by.
Eastward the dusk rain curtain hung,
and swiftly across it the rainbow sprung.

"Papa! Papa! What is it?" she cried
as she gazed with her blue eyes opened wide
at the wonderful arch that bridged the heaven
vividly glowing with colors—seven.

"Why that is the rainbow, darling child,"
and the father down on his baby smiled.
"What makes it, Papa?"
                        "The sun, my dear,
that shines on the water drops so clear."

Here was a beautiful mystery.
No more questions to ask had she.
But she thought the garden's loveliest flowers
had floated upward and caught in the showers—

Rose, violet, orange marigold
in a ribbon of light on the clouds unrolled.
Red of poppy, and green leaves too,
sunflower yellow, and larkspur blue.

A great wide wondrous, splendid wreath
it seemed to the little girl beneath.
How did it grow so fast up there
and suddenly blossom high in the air?

She could not take her eyes from the sight.
"Oh, look!" she cried in her deep delight
as she watched the glory spanning the gloom.
"Oh, look at the beautiful water bloom!"

FERN SEED

She filled her shoes with fern seed,
  this foolish little Nell,
and in the summer sunshine
  went dancing down the dell.
For who so treads on fern seed—
  so fairy stories tell—
becomes invisible at once
  so potent is its spell.

A frog mused by the brookside:
  "Can you see me?" she cried.
He leaped across the water,
  a flying leap, and wide.
Oh, that's because I asked him.
  I must not speak, she thought,
and skipping o'er the meadow,
  the shady wood she sought.

The squirrel chattered on the bough,
nor noticed her at all.
The birds sang high, the birds sang low,
with many a cry and call.
The rabbit nibbled in the grass;
the snake basked in the sun.
The butterflies, like floating flowers,
wavered and gleamed and shone.

The spider in his hammock swung,
the gay grasshoppers danced,
and now and then a cricket sung
and shining beetles glanced.
Twas all because the pretty child
so softly, softly trod—
You could not hear a footfall
upon the yielding sod.

But she was filled with such delight,
   this foolish little Nell.
And with her fern seed-laden shoes,
   danced back across the dell.
I'll find my mother now, she thought,
   What fun twill be to call,
'Mamma! Mamma!' while she can see
   no little girl at all.

She peeped in through the window—
   Mamma sat in a dream.
About the quiet sun-steeped house
   all things asleep did seem.
She stepped across the threshold.
   So lightly had she crept,
the dog upon the mat lay still
   and still the kitty slept.

Patient, beside her mother's knee
   to try her wondrous spell,
waiting she stood, till all at once
   waking, Mamma cried, "Nell!
where have you been? Why do you gaze
   at me with such strange eyes?"
"But can you see me, Mother dear?"
   poor Nelly, faltering, cries.

"See you? Why not, my little girl?
   Why should Mamma be blind?"
And pretty Nell unties her shoes
   with fairy fern-seed lined.
She tosses up into the air
   a little powdery cloud,
and frowns upon it as it falls,
   and murmurs half aloud:

"It wasn't true, a word of it—
   about the magic spell.
I never will believe again
   what fairy stories tell!"

THE PIMPERNEL

She walks beside the silent shore—
   the tide is high, the breeze is still.
No ripple breaks the ocean floor.
   The sunshine sleeps upon the hill.

The turf is warm beneath her feet,
   bordering the beach of stone and shell,
and thick about her path the sweet
   red blossoms of the pimpernel.

"Oh, sleep not yet, my flower!" she cries,
   "nor prophesy of storm to come.
Tell me that under steadfast skies
   fair winds shall bring my lover home."

She stoops to gather flower and shell.
   She sits, and smiling, studies each.
She hears the full tide rise and swell
   and whisper softly on the beach.

Waking, she dreams a golden dream,
   remembering with what still delight
to watch the sunset's fading gleam,
   here by the waves they stood last night.

She leans on that encircling arm
   divinely strong with power to draw
her nature, as the moon doth charm
   the swaying sea with heavenly law.

All lost in bliss the moments glide.
   She feels his whisper, his caress.
The murmur of the mustering tide
   brings her no presage of distress.

What breaks her dream? She lifts her eyes
   reluctant to destroy the spell.
The color from her bright cheek dies—
   Close folded is the pimpernel.

With rapid glance she scans the sky;
   rises a sudden wind and grows,
and charged with storm the cloud-heaps lie.
   Well may the scarlet blossoms close.

A touch, and bliss is turned to bale;
   life only keeps the sense of pain.
The world holds naught save one white sail
   flying before the wind and rain.

Broken upon the wheel of fear
   she wears the storm-vexed hour away,
and now in gold and fire draws near
   the sunset of her troubled day.

But to her sky is yet denied
   the sun that lights the world for her;
she sweeps the rose-flushed ocean wide
   with eager eyes, the quick tears blur—

and lonely, lonely all the space
   stretches with never sign of sail,
and sadder grows her wistful face;
   and all the sunset splendors fail.

And cold and pale in still despair
   with heavier grief than tongue can tell,
she sinks—upon her lips a prayer,
   her cheek against the pimpernel.

Bright blossoms wet with showery tears
   on her shut eyes their droplets shed.
Only the wakened waves she hears
   that, singing, drown his rapid tread.

"Sweet, I am here." Joy's gates swing wide
   and heaven is theirs, and all is well.
And left beside the ebbing tide,
   forgotten, is the pimpernel.

MILKING

Little dun cow to the apple tree tied,
   chewing the cud of reflection,
I that am milking you sit by your side
   lost in a sad retrospection.

Far o'er the field the tall daisies blush warm,
   for rosy the sunset is dying.
Across the still valley, o'er meadow and farm,
   the flush of its beauty is lying.

White foams the milk in the pail at my feet;
   clearly the robins are calling.
Soft blows the evening wind after the heat;
   cool the long shadows are falling.

Little dun cow, tis so tranquil and sweet.
   Are *you* light-hearted, I wonder?
What do *you* think about—something to eat?
   On clover and grass do you ponder?

I am remembering days that are dead
   and a brown little maid in the gloaming,
milking her cow with the west burning red
   over waves that about her were foaming.

Up from the sad east the deep shadows loomed
  out of the distance and found her.
Lightly she sang while the solemn sea boomed
  like a great organ around her.

Under the lighthouse no sweet briar grew.
  Dry was the grass, and no daisies
waved in the wind, and the flowers were few
  that lifted their delicate faces.

But oh, she was happy and careless and blest,
  full of the song sparrow's spirit;
grateful for life—for the least and the best
  of the blessings that mortals inherit.

Fairer than gardens of Paradise seemed
  the desolate spaces of water.
Nature was hers—clouds that frowned, stars that gleamed—
  What beautiful lessons they taught her.

Would I could find you again, little maid,
  striving with utmost endeavor—
could find in my breast that light heart, unafraid,
  that has vanished forever and ever.

IMPRISONED

ALL'S WELL

What dost thou here, young wife, by the waterside
  gathering crimson dulse?
Know'st thou not that the cloud in the west glooms wide
  and the wind has a hurrying pulse?

Peaceful the eastern waters before thee spread
  and the cliffs rise high behind
while thou gatherest seaweeds, green and brown and red,
  to the coming trouble, blind.

She lifts her eyes to the top of the granite crags
  and the color ebbs from her cheek.
Swift vapors scurry the black squall's tattered flags
  and she hears the gray gull shriek.

And like a blow is the thought of the little boat
  by this on its homeward way—
a tiny skiff like a cockle shell, afloat
  in the tempest threatened bay

with husband and brother who sailed away to the town
  when fair shone the morning sun,
to tarry but till the tide in the stream turned down,
  then seaward again to run.

Homeward she flies. The land breeze strikes her cold;
  a terror is in the sky.
Her little babe with his tumbled hair of gold
  in her mother's arms doth lie.

She catches him up with a breathless, questioning cry:
  "O Mother, speak! Are they near?"
"Dear, almost home. At the western window high
  thy father watches in fear."

She climbs the stair: "Oh Father, must they be lost?"
  He answers never a word.
Through the glass he watches the line the squall has crossed
  as if no sound he heard.

And the Day of Doom seems come in the angry sky,
    and a low roar fills the air.
In an awful stillness the dead-black waters lie,
    and the rocks gleam ghastly and bare.

Is it a snow-white gull's wing fluttering there
    in the midst of that hush of dread?
Ah no, tis the narrow strip of canvas they dart
    in the face of the storm to spread.

A moment more and all the furies are loose;
    the coast line is blotted out.
The skiff is gone, the rain-cloud pours its sluice
    and she hears her father shout:

"Down with your sail!"—as if through the tumult wild
    and the distance, his voice might reach.
And stunned, she clasps still closer her rosy child,
    bereft of speech.

But her heart cries low as writhing it lies on the rack.
"Sweet, art thou fatherless?"
And swift to her mother she carries the little one back,
where she waits in her sore distress.

Then into the heart of the storm she rushes forth.
Like leaden bullets the rain
beats hard in her face, and the hurricane from the north
would drive her back again.

It splits the shingles off the roof like a wedge.
It lashes her clothes and her hair.
But slowly she fights her way to the western ledge
with the strength of her despair.

Through the flying spray, through the rain-cloud's
                                    shattered stream,
what shapes in the distance grope
like figures that haunt the shore of a dreadful dream?
She is wild with a desperate hope.

Have pity, merciful Heaven, can it be?
   Is it no vision that mocks?
From billow to billow the headlong plunging sea
   has tossed them high on the rocks.

And the hollow skiff like a child's toy lies on the ledge
   this side of the roaring foam.
And up from the valley of death, from the grave's drear edge
   like ghosts of men they come.

Oh sweetly, sweetly shines the sinking sun,
   and the storm is swept away.
Piled high in the east are the cloud-heaps purple and dun,
   and peacefully dies the day.

But a sweeter peace falls soft on the grateful souls
   in the lonely isle that dwell.
And the whisper and rush of every wave that rolls
   seem murmuring, "All is well."

SLUMBER SONG

Thou little child with tender, clinging arms,
  drop thy sweet head, my darling, down and rest
upon my shoulder, rest with all thy charms.
  Be soothed and comforted; be loved and blessed.

Against thy silken honey-colored hair
  I lean a loving cheek, a mute caress.
Close, close I gather thee and kiss thy fair
  white eyelids, sleep so softly doth oppress.

Dear little face that lies in calm content
  within the gracious hollow that God made
in every human shoulder, where He meant
  some tired head for comfort should be laid.

Most like a heavy-folded rose thou art
  in summer air reposing, warm and still.
Dream thy sweet dreams upon my quiet heart.
  I watch thy slumber—naught shall do thee ill.

LAND-LOCKED

Black lie the hills; swiftly doth daylight flee,
   and, catching gleams of sunset's dying smile,
   through the dusk land for many a changing mile
the river runneth softly to the sea.

O happy river, could I follow thee;
   O yearning heart, that never can be still;
   O wistful eyes, that watch the steadfast hill longing for
level line of solemn sea!

Have patience; here are flowers and songs of birds,
   beauty and fragrance, wealth of sound and sight,
   all summer's glory thine from morn till night,
and life too full of joy for uttered words.

Neither am I ungrateful, but I dream
   deliciously how twilight falls tonight
   over the glimmering water, how the light
dies blissfully away, until I seem

to feel the wind, sea-scented, on my cheek,
  to catch the sound of dusky flapping sail
  and dip of oars, and voices on the gale
afar off, calling low—my name they speak.

O Earth! Thy summer song of joy may soar
  ringing to heaven in triumph. I but crave
  the sad, caressing murmur of the wave
that breaks in tender music on the shore.

IMPRISONED

Lightly she lifts the large, pure, luminous shell—
   poises it in her strong and shapely hand:
"Listen," she says, "it has a tale to tell
   spoken in language you may understand."

Smiling, she holds it at my dreaming ear.
   The old, delicious murmur of the sea
steals like enchantment through me, and I hear
   voices like echoes of eternity.

She stirs it softly. Lo, another speech.
   In one of its dim chambers shut from sight
is sealed the water that has kissed the beach
   where the far Indian Ocean leaps in light.

Those laughing ripples, hidden evermore
   in utter darkness, plaintively repeat
their lapsing on the glowing tropic shore
   in melancholy whispers low and sweet.

O prisoned wave that may not see the sun;
　O voice that never may be comforted;
you cannot break the web that fate has spun.
　Out of your world are light and gladness fled!

The red dawn nevermore shall tremble far
　across the leagues of radiant brine to you.
You shall not sing to greet the evening star
　nor dance exulting under heaven's clear blue.

Inexorably woven is the weft
　that shrouds from you all joy but memory.
Only this tender low lament is left
　of all the sumptuous splendor of the sea.

SONG

Past the point and by the beach
    (oh but the waves ran merrily
with laughter light and silver speech,
    and red the sunset flushed the sea)

two lovers wandered side by side—
    (oh but the waves ran merrily).
They watched the rushing of the tide,
    and fairer than a dream was she.

About her slender waist was cast
    (oh but the waves ran merrily)
his strong right arm that held her fast,
    a zone that clasped her royally.

He gazed in her bewildering face
    (oh but the waves ran merrily):
"See how the waves each other chase?
    So follow all my thoughts to thee."

"And seest thou yonder star," she said—
   (oh but the waves ran merrily)
"superb in yonder evening red?
   So dost thou light my life for me!"

Twas long ago that star did shine,
   (oh but the waves ran merrily).
Love made for them the world divine
   in that old time beside the sea.

The soft wind sighs, the great sea rolls,
   (oh but the waves run merrily).
What has time done with those two souls,
   and love who charmed them, where is he?

SONNET

Not so! You stand as long ago a king
  stood on the seashore, bidding back the tide
that onward rolled resistless still, to fling
  its awful volume landward, wild and wide.
And just as impotent is your command
  to stem the tide that rises in my soul.
It ebbs not at the lifting of your hand.
  It owns no curb; it yields to no control.
Mighty it is, and of the elements—
  Brother of winds and lightning, cold and fire;
subtle as light, as steadfast and intense;
  sweet as the music of Apollo's lyre.
You think to rule the ocean's ebb and flow
with that soft woman's hand? Nay, love, not so.

MIDSUMMER GLORIES

A THANKSGIVING

High on the ledge the wind blows the bayberry bright,
turning the leaves till they shudder and shine in the light.
Yellow St. John's-wort and yarrow are nodding their heads.
Iris and wild rose are glowing in purples and reds.

Swift flies the schooner careering beyond o'er the blue;
faint shows the furrow she leaves as she cleaves lightly through;
gay gleams the fluttering flag at her delicate mast;
full swell the sails with the wind that is following fast.

Quail and sandpiper and swallow and sparrow are here.
Sweet sound their manifold notes, high and low, far and near;
chorus of musical waters, the rush of the breeze
steady and strong from the south—What glad voices are these!

O cup of the wild rose, curved close to hold odorous dew,
what thought do you hide in your heart? I would that I knew.
O beautiful iris, unfurling your purple and gold,
what victory flings you abroad in the flags you unfold?

Sweet may your thought be, red rose, but still sweeter is mine
close in my heart hidden, clear as your dewdrop divine.
Flutter your gonfalons, iris, the paean I sing
is for victory better than joy or than beauty can bring.

Into thy calm eyes, O nature, I look and rejoice.
Prayerful, I add my one note to the Infinite voice
as shining and singing and sparkling glides on the glad day
and eastward the swift-rolling planet wheels into the gray.

SONG

A rushing of wings in the dawn;
  a flight of birds in the sky.
The darkness of night withdrawn
  in an outburst of melody.

O birds through the heaven that soar
  with such tumult of jubilant song!
The shadows are flying before,
  for the rapture of life is strong.

And my spirit leaps to the light
  on the wings of its hope new-born,
and I follow your radiant flight
  through the golden halls of morn.

THE NESTING SWALLOWS

The summer day was spoiled with fitful storm.
    At night the wind died and the soft rain dropped
with lulling murmur, and the air was warm.
    And all the tumult and the trouble stopped.

We sat within the bright and quiet room
    glowing with light and flowers and friendliness;
and faces in the radiance seemed to bloom
    touched into beauty as by a caress.

And one struck music from the ivory keys—
    Beethoven's music. And the awful chords
upbore us like the waves of mighty seas
    that sing aloud, "All glory is the Lord's!"

And the great sound awoke, beneath the eaves,
    the nestling swallows. And their twittering cry
with the light touch of raindrops on the leaves
    broke into the grand surging melody.

Across its deep tremendous questioning,
   its solemn acquiescence, low and clear,
the rippling notes ran sweet—with airy ring
   surprised, inquiring, but devoid of fear;

lapsing to silence at the music's close—
   a dreamy clamor, a contented stir.
"It made no discord," smiling as he rose,
   said the great master's great interpreter.

No discord, truly. Ever nature weaves
   her sunshine with her shadow, joy with pain:
the asking thunder through high heaven that cleaves
   is lost in the low ripple of the rain.

About the edges of the dread abyss
   the innocent blossoms laugh toward the sun.
Questions of life and death, of bale or bliss
   a thousand tender touches overrun.

Why should I chronicle so slight a thing?
  But such things light up life like wayside flowers,
and memory, like a bird with folded wing,
  broods with still joy o'er such delicious hours.

Dear unforgotten time. Fair summer night!
  Thy nestling swallows and thy dropping rain,
the golden music and the faces bright
  will steal with constant sweetness back again:

a joy to keep when winter darkness comes,
  a living sense of beauty to recall,
a warm bright thought when bitter cold benumbs,
  to make me glad and grateful. That is all.

MIDSUMMER MIDNIGHT

The wide still moonlit water miles away
   stretches in lonely splendor. Whispers creep
about us from the midnight wind, and play
   among the flowers that breathe so sweet in sleep.
A soft touch sways the milk-white stately phlox,
and on its slender stem the poppy rocks.

Fair faces turn to watch the dusky sea
   and clear eyes brood upon the path of light
the white moon makes, the while deliciously
   like some vague tender memory of delight,
or like some half-remembered dear regret,
rises the odor of the mignonette.

Midsummer glories: moonlight, flowers asleep,
   and delicate perfume; mystic winds that blow
soft-breathing full of balm, and the great deep
   in leagues of shadow swaying to and fro;
and loving human thought to mark it all,
and human hearts that to each other call—

Needs the enchantment of the summer night
   another touch to make it perfect? Hark
what sudden shaft of sound like piercing light
   strikes on the ear athwart the moonlit dark,
like some keen shock of joy is heard within
the wondrous music of the violin.

It is as if dumb nature found a voice
   and spoke with power, though in an unknown tongue.
What kinship has the music with the noise
   of waves or winds, or with the flowers slow-swung
like censers to and fro upon the air,
or with the shadow or the moonlight fair?

And yet it seems some subtle link exists—
   we know not how. And over every phase
of thought and feeling, wandering as it lists,
   playing upon us as the westwind plays
over the wind-harp, the subduing strain
sweeps with resistless power of joy and pain.

Slow ebbs the golden tide and all is still.
   Ask the magician at whose touch awoke
that mighty, penetrating, prisoned will—
   the matchless voice that so divinely spoke
kindling to fresher life the listening soul,
what daring thought such fire from heaven stole?

He cannot tell us how the charm was wrought
   though in his hand he holds the potent key;
nor read the spell that to the sweet night brought
   this crown of rapture and of mystery,
and lifted every heart, and drew away
all trace of worldliness that marred the day.

But every head is bowed. We watch the sea
   with other eyes, as if some hint of bliss
spoke to us through the yearning melody
   of glad new worlds, of brighter lives than this;
while still the milk-white stately phlox waves slow,
and drowsily the poppy rocks below.

THE HAPPY BIRDS

All about the gable tall, swift the swallows flit,
    wheel and call and dart and, fluttering, chatter sweet.
All along the sloping sunny eaves they perch and sit
    bright as lapis-lazuli glittering in the heat.

O spirits of the summer so dainty, delicate;
    creatures born of sunshine and cheer and all delight;
pray you, but delay a moment—yet a little wait
    ere for southern lands again you spread your wings in flight.

Yet the August sun is hot. Yet the days are long
    though the grass is over-ripe and the aster blows.
Still the silence echoes to the sparrow's quiet song;
    still, though late, in thorny thickets lingers the wild rose.

Tarry yet a little, for after you have flown,
    lonely, all the housetops, and still the air will grow.
Where your cheerful voices rang, autumn winds will moan—
    Presently we shall be dull with winter's weight of snow.

O that we could follow you and cling to summer's hand,
    ye happy, happy birds flying lightly through the sky—
reach with you the rapture of some far, sunny land;
    leave to winter's bitterness our glad and gay good-bye.

114

REMONSTRANCE

"Come out and hear the birds sing! Oh, wherefore sit you there
at the western window watching, dreamy-pale and still and fair
while the warm summer wind disparts your tresses' clustering gold?
What is it on the dim sea line your eyes would fain behold?"
  "I seek a sail that never looms from out the purple haze
  at rosy dawn, or fading eve, or in the noontide's blaze."

"A sail? Lo, many a column of white canvas far and near!
All day they glide across the blue, appear and disappear.
See, how they crowd the offing, flocking from the sultry South!
Why stirs a smile more sad than tears the patience of your mouth?"
  "They lean before the freshening breeze. They cross the ocean floor.
  But the ship that brings me tidings of my love comes never more."

"Come out into the garden where the crimson phloxes burn,
and every slender lily-stem upbears a lustrous urn.
A thousand greetings float to you from bud and bell and star.
Their sweetness freights the breathing wind; how beautiful they are."
  "Their brilliant color blinds me. I sicken at their breath.
  The whisper of this mournful wind is sad to me as death."

"And must you sit so white and cold while all the world is bright?
Ah, come with me and see how all is brimming with delight.
On the beach the emerald breaker murmurs o'er the tawny sand.
The white spray from the rock is tossed, by melting rainbows spanned.."
  "Nay, mock me not! I have no heart for nature's happiness.
    One sound alone my soul can fill, one shape my sight can bless."

"And are your fetters forged so fast though you were free and strong,
by the old mysterious madness, told in story and in song
since burdened with the human race the world began to roll?
Can you not thrust the weight away, so heavy on your soul?"
  "There is no power in earth or heaven such madness to destroy,
    and I would not part with sorrow that is sweeter far than joy."

"Oh marvelous content, that from such still despair is born.
Nay, I would wrestle with my fate 'till love were slain with scorn.
Oh mournful Mariana! I would never sit so pale,
watching with eyes grown dim with dreams, the coming of a sail."
  "Peace, peace. How can you measure a depth you never knew?
    My chains to me are dearer than your freedom is to you."

THE SPANIARDS' GRAVES
At the Isles of Shoals

O sailors, did sweet eyes look after you
  the day you sailed away from sunny Spain,
bright eyes that followed fading ship and crew
  melting in tender rain?

Did no one dream of that drear night to be,
  wild with the wind, fierce with the stinging snow,
when on yon granite point that frets the sea,
  the ship met her death blow?

Fifty long years ago these sailors died.
  (None know how many sleep beneath the waves.)
Fourteen gray headstones rising side by side
  point out their nameless graves.

Lonely, unknown, deserted, but for me
  and the wild birds that flit with mournful cry,
and sadder winds, and voices of the sea
  that moan perpetually.

Wives, mothers, maidens, wistfully in vain
   questioned the distance for the yearning sail
that, leaning landward, should have stretched again
   white arms wide on the gale

to bring back their beloved. Year by year,
   weary they watched, till youth and beauty passed
and lustrous eyes grew dim, and age drew near
   and hope was dead at last.

Still, summer broods o'er that delicious land,
   rich, fragrant, warm with skies of golden glow.
Live any yet of that forsaken band
   who loved so long ago?

O Spanish women over the far seas,
   could I but show you where your dead repose;
could I send tidings on this northern breeze
   that strong and steady blows!

Dear dark-eyed sisters, you remember yet
   these you have lost. But you can never know
one stands at their bleak graves whose eyes are wet
   with thinking of your woe.

THE GREAT BLUE HERON
A Warning

The great blue heron stood all alone
  by the edge of the solemn sea
on a broken boulder of gray trap stone.
  He was lost in a reverie.

And when I climbed the low rough wall
  at the top of the sloping beach
to gather the driftwood great and small
  left scattered to dry and bleach,

I saw, as if carved from the broken block
  on which he was standing, the bird
like a part of the boulder of blue-gray rock,
  for never a feather he stirred.

I paused to watch him. Below my breath:
  "Oh beautiful creature," I cried,
"Do you know you are standing here close to your death,
    by the brink of the quiet tide?

You cannot know of the being called Man!
    The lord of creation is he,
and he slays all earth's creatures wherever he can
    in the air or the land or the sea.

He's not a hospitable friend. If he sees
    some wonderful, beautiful thing
that runs in the woodland, or floats in the breeze
    on the banner-like breadth of its wing,

straight he goes for his gun, its sweet life to destroy
    for mere pleasure of killing alone.
He will ruin its beauty and quench all its joy
    though tis useless to him as a stone."

Then I cried aloud, "Fly, before over the sand
    this lord of creation arrives
with his shot and his powder and gun in his hand
    for the spoiling of innocent lives."

O, stately and graceful and slender and tall
   the heron stood silent and still
as if careless of warning and deaf to my call—
   unconscious of danger or ill.

"Fly! Fly to some lonelier place and fly fast,
   to the very North Pole—anywhere!"
Then he rose and soared high, and swept eastward at last
   trailing long legs and wings in the air.

"Now perhaps you may live and be happy," I said.
   "Sail away, beauty, fast as you can.
Put the width of the earth and the breadth of the sea
   betwixt you and the being called Man."

THE MINUTE GUNS

I stood within the little cove
   full of the morning's life and hope
while heavily the eager waves
   charged thundering up the rocky slope.

The splendid breakers. How they rushed
   all emerald green and flashing white,
tumultuous in the morning sun,
   with cheer and sparkle and delight.

And freshly blew the fragrant wind,
   the wild sea wind across their tops,
and caught the spray and flung it far
   in sweeping showers of glittering drops.

Within the cove all flashed and foamed
   with many a fleeting rainbow hue;
without, gleamed bright against the sky
   a tender wavering line of blue

where tossed the distant waves. And far
  shone silver-white a quiet sail,
and overhead the soaring gulls
  with graceful pinions stemmed the gale.

And all my pulses thrilled with joy
  watching the winds' and waters' strife—
with sudden rapture. And I cried,
  "Oh, sweet is life; thank God for life!"

Sailed any cloud across the sky
  marring this glory of the sun's?
Over the sea, from distant forts
  there came the boom of minute guns.

War tidings! Many a brave soul fled,
  and many a heart the message stuns.
I saw no more the joyous waves. . .
  I only heard the minute guns.

SONG

Rolls the long breaker in splendor and glances,
  leaping in light.
Sparkling and singing the swift ripple dances,
  laughing and bright.
Up through the heaven the curlew is flying,
  soaring so high.
Sweetly his wild notes are ringing and dying
  lost in the sky.
Glitter. The sails to the southwind careening,
  white-winged and brave,
bowing to breeze and to billow, and leaning
  low o'er the wave.
Beautiful wind with the touch of a lover
  leading the hours,
helping the winter-worn world to recover
  all its lost flowers.
Gladly I hear thy warm whisper of rapture,
  'Sorrow is o'er.'
Earth all her music and bloom shall recapture,
  happy once more.

FIRE & FRAGRANCE

TWO

She turned the letter's rustling page. Her smile
   made bright the air about her while she read:
"I come to you tomorrow, love. Meanwhile
   love me, my sweet," he said.

"What other business has my life?" she thought,
   and musing passed, as in some happy dream,
to the day's care and toils, and while she wrought
   time, winged with light did seem.

Tomorrow! When the summer morning broke
   in rose and gold and touched her slumbering eyes
softly with tempered splendor and she woke
   to the rich dawn's surprise,

birds sang aloft and roses bloomed below,
   flushed wide the tender fleecy mists above,
came memory, leading hope, and whispered low,
   "Love me. I come, my love."

"So that thou comest," she thought, "skies may grow gray.
  The sun may fade, the sea with foam blanch white.
Tempest and thunder dread may spoil the day
  but not my deep delight."

O sweet and awful Love. O Power Supreme,
  mighty and sacred. Terrible art thou!
Beside thee life and death are but a dream;
  before thee all must bow.

When in the west the sunset's crimson flame
  burned low and wasted, and the cool winds blew,
watching the steadfast sky she heard her name
  breathed in the voice she knew.

Joy shook her heart, nor would its pulse be stilled.
  Her fair cheek borrowed swift the sunset's bloom.
A presence beautiful and stately filled
  the silence of the room.

"Hast thou no word of welcome?" For indeed
  like some mute marble goddess proud stood she.
She turned. "Oh king of men," she cried, "what need
  that I should welcome thee?"

Her eyes divine beneath her solemn brows
  met his clear gaze and measured strength for strength.
She drooped, as to the sun the lily bows,
  into his arms at length.

Wide swung heaven's gates for them; no more they knew.
  The silent stars looked in. They saw them not.
The slow winds wandered soft through dusk and dew.
  But earth was all forgot.

SONG

I wore your roses yesterday
   about this light robe's folds of white.
Wherein their gathered sweetness lay,
   still clings their perfume of delight.

And all in vain the warm wind sweeps
   these airy folds like vapor fine.
Among them still the odor sleeps
   and haunts me with a dream divine.

So to my heart your memory clings,
   so sweet, so rich, so delicate.
Eternal summer-time it brings,
   defying all the storms of fate;

a power to turn the darkness bright
   till life with matchless beauty glows,
each moment touched with tender light,
   and every thought of you a rose.

AT DAWN

Early this morning, waking
   I heard the sandpipers call,
and the sea on the shore was breaking
   with a dreamy rise and fall.

The dawn that was softly blushing
   touched cloud and wave with rose,
and the sails in the west were flushing;
   no breeze stirred their repose.

What tone in the water's falling
   had reached me while I dreamed?
What sound in the wild birds' calling
   like a heavenly greeting seemed?

What meant the delicate splendor
   that brightened the conscious morn
with a radiance fresh and tender
   crowning the day newborn?

All nature's musical voices
    whispered, "Awake and see;
awake for the day rejoices."
    What news had the morn for me?

Then I remembered the blessing
    so sweet, Oh friend, so near;
the joy beyond all expressing—
    today you would be here.

IN SEPTEMBER

Leaping from the boat, through the lazy sparkling surf,
up the slope we press o'er the rich elastic turf.
Heavy waves the goldenrod in the morning breeze;
swift spring the startled grasshoppers, thick about our knees.

Look, how shines the distance! Leagues of water—blue,
wind-swept, sunshine-flooded, with a flying sail or two.
Gleaming white as silver, and dreaming, here and there,
a snowy-breasted gull gloats in the golden air.

How sweet to climb together the scented flowery slope,
oh dearest, hand in hand like children following hope;
laughing at the grasshoppers, singing with delight
only to be alive this September morning bright.

But where would be the beauty of this brilliant atmosphere
wert thou away, my darling? Would not the sky be drear,
and gray the living azure of the changing sparkling sea?
And blossoms, birds and sails and clouds;
what would they be to me?

Rest we here a little upon the breezy height
and watch the play of color, the shadow and the light;
and let the lovely moment overflow us with its bliss.
When shall we find another so beautiful as this?

I turn from all the splendor to those clear eyes of thine
that watch the shimmering sails on the far horizon line
while sun and wind salute thy cheek till roses blossom there,
thou golden creature, than the morn, a thousand times more fair.

Ah, must it end? Must winter hurl its snow across the sea
and roar with leagues of bitterness between thy face and me?
Must chill December fill with murk and storm this wooing air,
and the west wind wail like the voice of some supreme despair?

Too surely. But, oh friendly eyes, hold summer safe for me;
only, oh gentle heart, keep warm and sweet my memory,
and no fury of the tempest my world can desolate—
This winged joy will lift my soul above the storms of fate.

SONG

Love, art thou weary with the sultry day?
 Fain would I be the cool and delicate air
about the whiteness of thy brow to play
 and softly, lightly, stir thy cloudy hair.

Upon thy head doth the fierce winter smite,
 and shudderest thou in darkness cold to be?
I would I were the coming of the light,
 shelter, and radiant warmth to comfort thee.

I would be fire and fragrance, light and air—
 all gracious things that serve thee at thy need:
music, to lift thy heart above all care;
 the wise and charming book that thou dost read.

There is no power that cheers and blesses thee
 but I do envy it, beneath the sun.
Thy health, thy rest, thy refuge I would be—
 thy heaven on earth, thine every good in one.

REVERIE

The white reflection of the sloop's great sail
  sleeps trembling on the tide.
In scarlet trim her crew lean o'er the rail
  lounging on either side.

Pale blue and streaked with pearl the waters lie
  and glitter in the heat.
The distance gathers purple bloom where sky
  and glimmering coast-line meet.

From the cove's curving rim of sandy gray
  the ebbing tide has drained
where mournful, in the dusk of yesterday
  the curlew's voice complained.

Half lost in hot mirage the sails afar
  lie dreaming, still and white.
No wave breaks; no wind breathes, the peace to mar.
  Summer is at its height.

How many thousand summers thus have shone
  across the ocean waste
passing in swift succession one by one,
  by the fierce winter chased.

The gray rocks blushing soft at dawn and eve,
  the green leaves at their feet,
the dreaming sails, the crying birds that grieve,
  ever themselves repeat.

And yet how dear and how forever fair
  is nature's friendly face.
And how forever new and sweet and rare,
  each old familiar grace.

What matters it that she will sing and smile
  when we are dead and still?
Let us be happy in her beauty while
  our hearts have power to thrill.

Let us rejoice in every moment bright,
  grateful that it is ours;
bask in her smiles with ever fresh delight,
  and gather all her flowers—

for presently we part. What will avail
  her rosy fires of dawn,
her noontide pomps, to us who fade and fail,
  our hands from hers withdrawn?

TO J. G. W.
On His Seventy-fifth Birthday

What is there left, I wonder,
  to give thee on this glad day?
Vainly I muse and ponder;
  what is there left to say?

There is winter abroad, and snow,
  and winds that are chill and drear
over the sad earth blow
  like the sighs of the dying year.

But the land thou lovest is warm
  at heart with the love of thee
and breaks into bloom and charm
  and fragrance, that thou mayest see.

Violet, laurel, and rose,
   they are laid before thy feet;
and the red rose deeper glows
   at a fate so proud and sweet.

Gifts and greeting and blessing,
   honor and praise, are thine.
There's naught left worth expressing
   by any word or sign.

So, like the rest, I offer
   the gift all gifts above
that heaven or earth can proffer—
   deep, gentle, grateful love.

HOMAGE

Nay, comrade, tis a weary path we tread
   through this world's desert spaces, dull and dry.
And long ago died out youth's morning-red;
   and low the sunset fires before us lie.

And you are worn, though brave the face you wear.
   Forbear the deprecating gesture, take
the honest admiration that I bear
   your genius, and be mute, for friendship's sake.

Up to your lips I lift a generous wine—
   pure, perfumed, potent, living, sparkling bright;
a deep cup, brimming with a draught divine.
   Drink, then, and be refreshed with my delight.

It gladdens you; you know the gift sincere;
   you dreamed not life yet held a thing so sweet?
Nay, noble friend, your thanks I will not hear;
   but I shall cast my roses at your feet

and go my way rejoicing that tis I
   who recognize, acknowledge, judge you best—
proud that a star so steadfast lights the sky,
   and in the power of blessing, you most blest.

A SONG OF HOPE

The morning breaks, the storm is past. Behold,
   along the west the lift grows bright—the sea
leaps sparkling blue to catch the sunshine's gold,
   and swift before the breeze the vapors flee.

Light cloud flocks white that troop in joyful haste
   up and across the pure and tender sky;
light laughing waves that dimple all the waste
   and break upon the rocks and hurry by.

Flying of sails, of clouds, a tumult sweet;
   wet tossing buoys, a warm wild wind that blows
the pennon out and rushes on to greet
   thy lovely cheek and heighten its soft rose.

Beloved, beloved! Is there no morning breeze
   to clear our sky and chase our mists away,
like this great air that sweeps the freshening seas,
   and wakes the old sad world to glad new day?

Sweeter than morning, stronger than the gale,
   deeper than ocean, warmer than the sun,
my love shall climb, shall claim thee, shall prevail
   against eternal darkness, dearest one.

MURDER STALKS UNHINDERED

TRUST

See how the wind is hauling point by point to the south
  by the boats in the little harbor that swing to its lightest touch.
And the coasting craft emerge from the far-off river's mouth,
  and on the rocks the breakers relax their impotent clutch.

At last is the tempest ended; the bitter northeast appeased.
  And the world will soon be sparkling in clear white fire and dew,
and the sullen clouds melt swiftly, by the might of warm wind seized,
  and the heavens shine in splendor, where broadens the
                             matchless blue.

Carol—the birds in chorus; glitters—the snow-white gull
  screaming loud in mid-air, slow-soaring high with delight.
And the rosebuds loosen their petals, the drenched flowers,
                             sodden and dull,
break out into stars of purple and gold and crimson and white.

Where wert thou, spirit of beauty, while earth lay cold and dark,
 and the chill wind struck to our hearts, and the sky like an enemy
and we crept through the mists desponding, and never
          a glimmering spark
 shot a ray through the gloom while the storm like a demon
          groveled and growled?

Where art thou, Heavenly Father, when thy world seems
         spoiled with sin,
 and darker far than thy tempest arises the smoke of doubt
that blackens the sky of the soul? For faith is hard to win.
 To our finite sight, wrong triumphs and noble things die out

while shapes of monstrous evil make fearful thy nights and days.
 And murder stalks unhindered, working its hideous will—
And innocence, gentleness, charity seem to forsake earth's ways;
 and in the hearts of thy creatures are madness and nameless ill.

Behind the cloud Thou waitest, hidden, yet very near,
 Infinite spirit of beauty, Infinite power of good.
At last Thou wilt scatter the vapors, and all things shall be clear;
 and evil shall vanish away, like a mist by the wind pursued.

ELIZA LAIGHTON

IMPATIENCE
E.L. (Eliza Laighton)

Only to follow you, dearest, only to find you.
　Only to feel for one instant the touch of your hand.
Only to tell you once of the love you left behind you—
　to say the world without you is like a desert of sand:

that the flowers have lost their perfume, the rose its splendor,
　and the charm of nature is lost in a dull eclipse;
that joy went out with the glance of your eyes so tender,
　and beauty passed with the lovely smile on your lips.

I did not dream it was you who kindled the morning
　and folded the evening purple in peace so sweet.
But you took the whole world's rapture without a warning,
　and left me naught save the print of your patient feet.

I count the days and the hours that hold us asunder.
　I long for death's friendly hand which shall rend in twain
with the glorious lightning flash and the golden thunder,
　these clouds of the earth, and give me my own again.

HER MIRROR

O mirror, whence her lovely face
    was wont to look with radiance sweet,
hast thou not kept of her some trace,
    some memory that thou mayest repeat?

Could I but find in thee once more
    some token of her presence dear.
O mirror, wilt thou not restore
    her shadow for an instant here?

Thou couldst not yield a boon so great.
    I see my own dim face and eyes
with love and longing desolate,
    all drowned in wistful memories.

Blindly for her dear hand I grope.
    There's nothing life can have in store
so sweet to me as this sweet hope
    to feel her smile on me once more.

GRANNA, DEAR

RUTH

A baby girl not two years old
   among the phlox and pansies stands,
and full of flowers as they can hold
   her mother fills her little hands

and bids her cross to where I stay
   within my garden's fragrant space
and guides her past the poppies gay
   'mid mazes of the blooming place

saying: "Go carry Thea these."
   Delighted, forth the baby fares
between the fluttering-winged sweet peas;
   her treasured buds she safely bears.

Tis but a step, but oh what stress
   of care. What difficulties wait.
How many pretty dangers press
   upon the path from gate to gate!

But high above her sunny head
   she tries the roses, sweet to hold—
now caught in coreopsis red,
   half wrecked upon a marigold,

or tangled in a cornflower tall,
   or hindered by the poppy tops—
she struggles on, nor does she fall,
   nor stalk nor stem her progress stops

until at last, the trials past,
   victorious o'er the path's alarms,
herself, her flowers, and all are cast
   breathless into my happy arms.

My smiling, rosy little maid—
   And while her joy-flushed cheek I kiss
and close to mine its bloom is laid
   I think, "So may you find your bliss

my precious. When in coming years
   life's path grows a bewildering maze,
so may you conquer doubts and fears
   and safely thread its devious ways

and find yourself all dangers past,
   clasped to a fonder breast than mine,
and gain your heavenly joy at last
   safe in the arms of love divine."

A POPPY SEED

"Tell you a story, my beautiful dear,
  of nixies, and pixies, and fairies with wings?
Well, curl up close in the corner here,
  and I'll show you more astonishing things.

I give you this small white packet to hold.
  'It rustles,' you say. Both the ends are sealed.
Patience a moment and you shall be told
  of the hundreds of captives that lie concealed

in this little paper. 'What? Living things?'
  Yes, full of life. 'Won't I take one out?'
Yes—only be careful. They have no wings
  but your lightest breathing will blow them about.

There, one in your warm pink palm I lay.
  You hardly can see it; 'does anything hide
in that wee atom of dust?' you say.
  Yes, wonderful glory is folded inside:

robes, my dear, that are fit for kings,
    scarlet splendor that dazzles the eyes;
buds, flowers, leaves, stalks—so many things.
    You look in my face with doubting surprise

and ask, 'Is it really, truly true?'
    No fairy story at all this time.
Don't you remember the poppy that grew
    at the foot of the trellis where sweet peas climb—

last summer close to the doorstep, where
    you and I loved to sit in the sun
and see the butterflies float in the air
    when the long bright day was almost done?

Don't you remember what joy we had
    watching that poppy grow high and higher
in its lovely gray-green garments clad,
    till the buds one evening showed streaks of fire,

and next day—oh it was all ablaze!
    Three or four flowers at once outburst
in the early sun's low, golden rays—
    and you were down at the doorstep first.

And what magnificence met our sight.
　What a heavenly time we had, we two,
just adoring it, lost in delight—
　for the gray-green leaves were spangled with dew

and the flowers, like banners of silken flames
　unfurled, stood each on its slender stem
while the soft breeze over them went and came,
　lightly and tenderly rocking them.

Dearest, don't you remember it all?
　How still it was. Not a whisper of sound
till a bird sang out from the garden wall
　and you slid from the step and stood on the ground,

and the poppy was higher than your bright head.
　Gently downward, one flower you bent
to see, in the midst of its burning red
　the delicate greens in a glory blent.

Bronze-green pollen on glowing rays
　from a center of palest emerald light
in a brilliant halo beneath our gaze—
　You haven't forgotten that exquisite sight?

No, indeed. I was sure of it. Well,
   all that perfection of shape and hue,
that wealth of beauty no tongue can tell
    lies hid in this seed I have given to you.

Just such a speck in the friendly ground
   I planted last May by the doorstep wide.
The self-same marvel that then we found,
    this atom of dust holds shut inside.

You can't believe it? But all are there:
   leaves, roots, flowers, stalks, color, and glow.
Tell me a story that can compare
    with this for a wonder—if any you know!"

MY HOLLYHOCK

I

Ah me, my scarlet hollyhock
whose stately head the breezes rock.
How sad, that in one night of frost
thy radiant beauty shall be lost,
and all thy glory overthrown
ere half thy ruby buds have blown.
All day across my window low
thy flowery stalk sways to and fro
against a background of blue sea.
On the south wind to visit thee
come airy shapes in sumptuous dyes:
rich golden, black-edged butterflies,
and humming-birds in emerald coats
with flecks of fire upon their throats
that in the sunshine whir and glance
and probe the flowers with slender lance,
and many a drunken drowsy bee
singing his song hilariously.
About the garden fluttering yet
in amber plumage streaked with jet
the gold finches charm all the air

151

with sweet sad crying everywhere.
To the dry sunflower stalks they cling
and on the ripened disks they swing;
with delicate delight they feed
on the rich store of milky seed.

II

Autumn goes loitering through the land,
a torch of fire within her hand.
Soft sleeps the bloomy haze that broods
o'er distant hills and mellowing woods.
Rustle the cornfields far and near,
and nuts are ripe and pastures sere,
and lovely odors haunt the breeze
borne o'er the sea and through the trees.
Belated beauty lingering still
so near the edge of winter's chill,
the deadly daggers of the cold
approach thee, and the year grows old.
Is it because I love thee so
thou waitest, waving to and fro
thy flowery spike to gladden me
against the background of blue sea?
I wonder—hast thou not some sense,

some measure of intelligence
responding to my joy in thee?
Almost, I dream that it may be.
Such subtleties are nature's, hid
her most well-trodden paths, amid.
Such sympathies along her nerves,
such sweetness in her fine reserves.
Howe'er it be, I thank the powers
that gave me such enchanted hours
this late October—watching thee
wave thy bright flowers against the sea.

SIR WILLIAM PEPPERRELL'S WELL
Isles of Shoals, 1790-1892 *

Little maid Margaret and I,
all in the sweet May weather,
roamed merrily and peacefully
the island slopes together.

The sun was midway in the west
that golden afternoon.
The sparrow sat above his nest
and sang his friendly tune.

The sky was clear; the sea was calm.
The wind blew from the south
and touched us with a breath of balm
and kissed her happy mouth.

The joyful, smiling little maid,
her pretty hand in mine—
"Look, Thea, at the flowers," she said.
"See how the eye-brights shine."

Scattered like pearls all milky fair
where'er our feet were set,
they glimmered, swayed by gentle air,
for little Margaret.

And here the crowfoot's gold was spilled,
and there the violet
its cream-white buds with fragrance filled—
and all for Margaret.

I took a grassy path that led
into a rocky dell.
"Come, and I'll show you, dear," I said,
"Sir William Pepperrell's well."

In the deep shadow of the rock
the placid water hid,
and seemed the sky above to mock
arums and ferns, amid.

"Is this Sir William Pepperrell's well?
But Thea, who was he?"
    "A nobleman, the records tell,
        a lord of high degree."

"And did he live here?"
                        "Sometimes, yes.
Yonder his house stood, dear.
By all the scattered stones, you'd guess
a dwelling once stood here.

There lie the doorsteps large and square
where feet went out and in
long years ago. A broken stair;
and here, the walls begin."

"How long ago did they live here?"
gravely the small maid spoke.
    "And tell me, did you know them, Thea—
        Sir William Pepperrell's folk?"

"A hundred years they have been dead.
No dear, we never met!"
  "But Thea, you're so old," she said,
  "You know you might forget. . .

    I'm only six. I'm very new;
    I can't remember much."
She clasped me as she nearer drew
with light and gentle touch.

  "Tell me, where are they now?" asked she.
(Oh question, ages old.)
"That, Margaret, is a mystery
no mortal has been told.

Here stood the house; there lies the well,
and nothing more we know
except that history's pages tell
they lived here long ago."

With serious eyes she gazed at me
and for a moment's space
a shadow of perplexity
flitted across her face.

Then, dancing down the sunlit way
she gathered bud and bell,
and 'mid its ferns, forgotten lay
Sir William Pepperrell's well.

* *Archeologists attribute the building of William*
Pepperrell's house on Hog Island (Appledore) to the mid-
1670s. His famous son, Sir William Pepperrell, lived on
the mainland in Kittery, and died in 1759 . The date 1892
probably refers to the year Celia wrote this poem. The
provenance of the first date, however, is unclear.

APPEAL

The childish voice rose to my ear
   sweet toned and eager, praying me,
"I am so little, Granna dear.
   Please lift me up so I can see."

I looked down at the pleading face,
   felt the small hand's entreating touch,
and stooping, caught in swift embrace
   the baby boy I loved so much,

and held him high that he might gaze
   at the great pageant of the sky,
the glory of the sunset's blaze,
   the glittering moon that curved on high.

With speechless love I clasped him close
   and read their beauty in his eyes,
and on his fair cheek kissed the rose,
   sweeter than blooms of Paradise.

And in my heart his eager prayer
   found echo, and the self-same cry
rose from my heart through heaven's air,
   "O gracious Father, lift me high.

So little and so low am I.
   Among earth's mists I call to Thee—
Show me the glory of Thy sky.
   Oh, lift me up that I may see!"

A HUMAN LIFETIME

STARLIGHT

The chill sad evening wind of winter blows
　across the headland bleak and bare and high
rustling the thin, dry grass that sparsely grows,
　and shivering, whispers like a human sigh.

The sky is thick with stars that sparkle keen,
　and great Cappella in the clear northeast
rolls slowly up the cloudless heaven serene,
　and the stern uproar of the sea has ceased

a fleeting moment, and the earth seems dead—
　So still, so sad, so lonely, and so cold.
Snow-dust beneath me, and above my head
　star-dust in blackness, like thick-sprinkled gold.

The stars of fire, the tiny stars of ice.
　The awful whirling worlds in space that wheel,
the dainty crystal's delicate device—
　One hand has fashioned both. And I, who kneel

here on this winter night twixt stars and snow,
    as transient as a snowflake and as weak,
yearning like all my fellow-men to know
    His hidden purpose that no voice may speak—

In silent awe I watch His worlds. I see
    mighty Cappella's signal, and I know
the steady beam of light that reaches me
    left the great orb full seventy years ago.

A human lifetime! Reason strives in vain
    to grasp at time and space, and evermore
thought, weary grown and baffled, must again
    retrace its slow steps to the humble door

of wistful patience; there to watch and wait
    devoutly till at last death's certain hand,
imperious, opens wide the mystic gate
    between us and the future He has planned.

Yea, death alone. But shall death conquer all?
  Love fights and pleads in anguish of despair.
Sooner shall great Cappella wavering fall
  than any voice respond to his wild prayer.

And yet, what fire divine makes hope to glow
  through the pale ashes of our earthly fate?
Immortal hope, above all joy, below
  all depths of pain wherein we strive, and wait.

Dull is our sense. Hearing we do not hear,
  and seeing see not; yet we vaguely feel
somewhere is comfort in the darkness drear.
  And hushing doubts and fears, we learn to kneel.

Starlight and silence; dumb are sky and sea.
  Silent as death the awful spaces lie.
Speechless, the bitter wind blows over me,
  sad as the breathing of a human sigh.

REMEMBRANCE

Fragrant and soft the summer wind doth blow.
  Weary I lie, with heavy half-shut eyes
  and watch, while wistful thoughts within me rise—
the curtain idly swaying to and fro.

There comes a sound of household toil from far:
  a woven murmur—voices shrill and sweet,
  clapping of doors and restless moving feet,
and tokens faint, of fret, and noise, and jar.

Without, the broad earth shimmers in the glare
  through the clear noon; high rides the blazing sun.
  The birds are hushed. The cricket's chirp alone
with tremulous music cleaves the drowsy air.

I think . . . past the gray rocks the wavelets run;
  the gold-brown seaweed drapes the ragged ledge.
  And brooding, silent at the water's edge,
the white gull sitteth shining in the sun.

THE SUNRISE NEVER FAILED US YET

Upon the sadness of the sea
the sunset broods regretfully.
From the far lonely spaces, slow
withdraws the wistful afterglow.

So out of life the splendor dies.
So darken all the happy skies.
So gathers twilight, cold and stern.
But overhead the planets burn.

And up the east another day
shall chase the bitter dark away.
What though our eyes with tears be wet?
The sunrise never failed us yet.

The blush of dawn may yet restore
our light and hope and joy once more.
Sad soul, take comfort, nor forget
that sunrise never failed us yet.

AN ISLAND GARDEN

Preface

Prior to the turn of the twentieth century, New England was experiencing a horticultural and formal gardening renaissance. Artists visiting the renowned sculptor Augustus Saint-Gaudens in Cornish, New Hampshire, strolled through elaborate Pan Gardens replete with marble benches and fountains, gold statuary, and high clipped juniper hedges. Mansions in Newport, Rhode Island, were landscaped with exotic tropical plants, tea houses, exquisite rose gardens, topiary, espaliered arbors, and intricate boxwood mazes.

Celia Thaxter's island garden fronting the piazza of her Appledore Island cottage hardly resembled the neat beds and ornately bordered pathways of these private summer residences. But the parade of color she managed to keep blooming from early spring to late fall on the small slope facing the sea gained quite a reputation.

From the moment she patted marigold seeds into the sparse soil when she was growing up on White Island, Celia had been captivated by the sprouting and blooming of flowers. And as she learned the craft of the pen, she continued to wield a garden trowel, gaining expertise in both these arts.

The first seeds for AN ISLAND GARDEN were sown by friends and mainland gardeners anxious to know some of

169

Celia's gardening secrets. One of the talented young artists who set up his easel beneath the hop vines at her summer colony seemed the perfect candidate to illustrate the book. For nearly a decade Childe Hassam had been filling his portfolio with watercolor sketches of Celia, her garden and salon, and of the Shoals seascape. AN ISLAND GARDEN with 21 illustrations by Hassam, was published in the spring of 1894, half a year before Celia's death. The cloth volume embossed in gold was divided into six unnumbered, untitled sections, each introduced by an emblematic flower "headpiece" designed and painted by Childe Hassam. The popularity of the book enhanced the young artist's career and established Celia's protégé as one of America's most gifted impression-istic painters.

Once in awhile Celia pays homage to naturalists and friends, quoting Charles Dudley Warner, Juliana Horatia Ewing, and other obscure authorities. She quotes from John Ruskin's long discourse on poppies and follows it with a few of her own lucid observations. Obviously, the vener-able British author has nothing on Celia when it comes to flowers. For Celia Thaxter is a gardener ahead of her time. She suggests that seed packagers should include packet information on soil types and weather. From an old piece of carpet she invents a portable knee-elbow pad for weeding. And when her garden is infested by aphids and other pests, she imports frogs (not native to the Isles), relying on the natural food chain rather than pesticide control. To the wonderment of friends, she talks to her plants: "reasoning and remonstrating with them. . . We are on such good terms, my flowers and I," she writes. Nearly a century later studies corroborate what the island gardener knew instinctively, that plants grow faster when they are talked to or music is played to them.

Celia took her garden inside too, cutting flowers at dawn and arranging them lovingly in myriad vases adorning every inch of space in her cottage salon. She often wore white, gray and other basic colors to offset a boutonniere or flower corsage, noting that nature often wore a spot of color, like the scarlet pimpernel growing from the cleft in a rock.

This brief excerpt from the original 126-page book focuses more on the "how to" aspects of her gardening. Birds, butterflies, island flora and fauna, and the other subjects which invariably crowd into Thaxter's prose give way to a seasonal journal recounting the successes and failures of her island garden. In one amusing passage, the island gardener can't sleep for fear the baby slugs are devouring her baby sweet peas. During the middle of the night she hastens from her bed to the garden and hoses off the leaves. In another episode, Celia ranges all over Appledore Island with a wheelbarrow looking for old stalks to use as garden stakes. Fall finds her lugging flats, pots, and bushels of plants to the steamer wharf for transport to Portsmouth where she's spending the winter.

Celia Thaxter's commitment and knowledge of gardening and writing have combined to make this book an American classic. Houghton Miffllin has printed a facsimile edition of the original, and it's a delight to read from cover to cover.

AN ISLAND GARDEN

In response to the many entreaties of strangers as well as friends who have said to me summer after summer, "Tell us how you do it. Write a book about it and tell us how it is done that we may go also and do likewise," I have written this book at last. Truly it contains the fruit of much sweet and bitter experience. Of what I speak I know, and of what I know I have freely given. I trust it may help the patient gardener to a reasonable measure of success, and to that end I have spared no smallest detail that seemed to me necessary, no suggestion that might prove helpful.

This little island garden of mine is so small that the amount of pure delight it gives in the course of a summer is something hardly to be credited. It lies along the edge of a piazza forty or fifty feet long, sloping to the south not more than fifteen feet wide, sheltered from the north winds and open to the sun. The whole piazza is thickly draped with vines: Hops, Honeysuckles, blue and white Clematis, Cinnamon vine (*Mina Lobata*), Nasturtiums, Morning glories, Japanese Hops, Woodbine, and the beautiful and picturesque Wild Cucumber (*Echinocystus Lobata*) which in July nearly smothers everything else and clothes

173

itself in a veil of filmy white flowers in loose clusters, fragrant, but never too sweet, always refreshing and exquisite. The vines make a grateful green shade, doubly delightful for that there are no trees on my island; and the shade is most welcome in the wide brilliancy of sea and sky.

———

Often I hear people say, "How do you make your plants flourish like this?" as they admire the little flower patch I cultivate in summer or the window gardens that bloom for me in the winter; "I can never make my plants blossom like this! What is your secret?" And I answer with one word: "Love." For that includes all—the patience that endures continual trial, the constancy that makes perseverance possible, the power of foregoing ease of mind and body to minister to the necessities of the thing beloved, and the subtle bond of sympathy which is as important, if not more so, than all the rest. For though I cannot go so far as a witty friend of mine who says that when he goes out to sit in the shade on his piazza, his Wistaria vine leans toward him and lays her head on his shoulder, I am fully and intensely aware that plants are conscious of love and respond to it as they do to nothing else.

———

When the snow is still blowing against the window pane in January and February and the wild winds are howling without, what pleasure it is to plan for summer that is to be.

Small shallow wooden boxes are ready, filled with mellow earth (of which I am always careful to lay in a supply before the ground freezes in the autumn) sifted and made damp; into it the precious seeds are dropped with a loving hand.

The boxes of seeds are put in a warm, dark place, for they only require heat and moisture till they germinate. Then, when the first precious green leaves begin to appear, what a pleasure it is to wait and tend on the young growths which are moved carefully to some cool, sunny chamber window in a room where no fire is kept. (For heat becomes the worst enemy at this stage, and they spindle and dwindle if not protected from it.) When they are large enough, having attained to their second leaves, each must be put into a little pot or egg shell by itself (all except the Poppies and their companions already in egg shells), so that by the time the weather is warm enough they will be ready to be set out, stout and strong, for early blooming.

This pleasant business goes on during the winter in the picturesque old town of Portsmouth, New Hampshire, whither I repair in the autumn from the Isles of Shoals—remaining through the cold weather and returning to the islands on the first of April. My upper windows all winter are filled with young Wallflowers, Stocks, single Dahlias, Hollyhocks, Poppies, and many other garden plants which are watched and tended with the most faithful care till the time comes for transporting them over the seas to Appledore. A small steam tug, the Pinafore, carries me and my household belongings over to the islands. And a pretty sight is the little vessel when she starts out from the old brown wharves and steams away down the beautiful Piscataqua River with her hurricane deck aweave with green leaves and flowers, for all the world like a May Day procession. My blossoming house plants go also and there are Palms and Ferns and many other lovely things that make the small boat gay indeed. All the boxes of sprouted seedlings are carefully packed in wide square baskets to keep them steady, and the stout young plants hold up their strong stems and healthy green leaves and take the wind and sun bravely as the vessel goes tossing over the salt waves out to sea.

So deeply is the gardener's instinct implanted in my soul, I really love the tools with which I work. The iron fork, the spade, the hoe, the rake, the trowel, and the watering pot are pleasant objects in my eyes. The ingenuity of modern times has invented many variations of these primitive instruments of toil and many of them are most useful and helpful, as, for instance, a short, five-pronged hand fork—a delightful tool to use in breaking up the earth about the roots of weeds. Some of the weeds are so wide-spreading and tenacious (like Clover and Mallow) that they seem to have fastened themselves around the nether millstone it is so difficult to disengage their hold. Once loosened, however, by the friendly little fork, they must come up whether they will or no.

I like to take the hoe in my hands and break to pieces the clods of earth left by the overturning spade, to work into the soil the dark velvet-smooth, scentless barn manure which is to furnish the best of food for my flowers. It is a pleasure to handle the light rake, drawing it evenly through the soil and combing out every stick and stone and straw and lump, till the ground is as smooth and fine as meal. This done carefully and thoroughly—the beds laid out neatly with their surface level as a floor and not heaped high enough to let the rains run off—then is the ground ready for the sowing of the seeds.

. . .If any seedsman would like to make his fortune without delay, he has only to have printed on every packet of seed he offers for sale the kind of soil, the food required by each plant.

For instance, why not say of Mignonette: It flourishes best in a poor and sandy soil. So treated, it is much more fragrant than in a rich earth which causes it to run to leaves and makes its flowers fewer and less sweet. Or of Poppies: Plant them in a rich sandy loam, all except the Californias (*Eschscholtzia*), which do best in a poor soil. Or of Pansies: Give them the richest earth you can find, no end of water, and partial shade. Or: Don't worry over drought for your Nasturtiums. They come from Chile and will live and thrive with less water than almost anything else that grows. Don't trouble yourself to enrich the ground for them. That makes them profuse, and coarse of leaves, and sparing of flowers. Leave them to shift for themselves (once having cleared them of weeds). No flower bears neglect so well. Or: Give your Zinnias a heavy soil; they like clay. Or: Keep Sweet Peas as wet as you can and make the ground for them as rich as possible. Or: Keep barn manure away from your Lilies for your life! They will not brook contact with it, but a rich soil they also like. Only, it must be made so by anything rather than stable manure. And they too like clay. They blossom best when it is given them. But transport to your garden a portion of the very barnyard itself in which to set Roses, Sunflowers and Hollyhocks, Honeysuckles and Dahlias.

Hints of this kind would be to the unaccustomed tiller of the soil simply invaluable. How much they would lessen failures and discouragements! And to learn these things by one's self takes half a lifetime of sad experience.

I copy the notes of a few days' work in the garden in May [and June] just to give an idea of their character and of the variety of occupation in this small space of ground.

May 11th: This morning at four o'clock the sky was one

rich red blush in the east over a sea as calm as a mirror. How could I wait for the sun to lift its scarlet rim above the dim sea line (though it rose punctually at forty-seven minutes past four), when my precious flower beds were waiting for me! It was not possible.

. . . All the boxes and baskets of the more delicate seedlings were to be put out from my chamber window on flat house-top and balcony, they and the forest of Sweet Peas to be thoroughly watered, and the Pansies half shaded with paper lest the sun should work them woe. At five the household was stirring; there was time to write a letter or two. Then came breakfast before six. And by half past six I was out of doors at work in the vast circle of motionless silence, for the sea was too calm for me to hear even its breathing. It was so beautiful—the dewy quiet, the freshness, the long still shadows, the matchless delicate sweet charm of the newly wakened world. Such a color as the grass had taken on during the last few warm days; and where the early shadows lay long across it, such indescribably richness of tone. There was so much for me to do I hardly knew where to begin.

May 12th: Again a radiant day. I watched the thin white half ring of the waning moon as it stole up the east through the May haze at dawn. This kind of haze belongs especially to this month. It is such an exquisite color like ashes of roses till the sun suffuses it with a burning blush before he

179

leaps alive from the ocean's rim. Again in the garden at a little after six—to find the sparrows busy tunneling up and down the bank devouring the Poppies that I planted yesterday. How they can see the seeds at all or why they should care to feast on anything so small or why they do not all perish (as poor Pillicoddy proposed doing from the effects of such doses of opium) passes my understanding. There was nothing to be done but to plant them all over and then trail through the dewy grass long boards to lay up and down, covering the bank for protection.

. . . All the rest of this day was spent in transplanting Asters from boxes into the beds all over the garden, edging nearly every bed with them so that when the fleeting glory of Poppies and other earlier annuals is gone, there will still be beautiful color to gladden our eyes late in the summer, quite into the autumn days.

In the afternoon I had all the many boxes of Sweet Peas brought to the piazza to be ready for transplanting, but remembering the sparrows, I covered each box carefully with mosquito netting before leaving them for the night.

May 15th: All along the piazza are the house plants waiting to be attended to, cut back, repotted, and the soil enriched for winter blooming. Every day I attend to them, a few at a time. I cannot spare much time from my planting, weeding, watering, transplanting and so forth in the garden, but soon they will be all done. Began to transplant a few of the hundreds of the main body of Sweet Pea plants into the ground, carefully covering each bed as I finished with breadths of light mosquito netting to make them sparrow-proof. As I was working busily I heard the sweet calling of curlews and looking up, saw six of them wheeling overhead.

May 20th: All the past days have been filled with transplanting and the most vigorous weeding. In these five days the Sweet Peas have grown so tall I was obliged to go after sticks for them today, wheeling my light wheelbarrow up over the hill and across the island toward the south, where among the old ruined walls of cellars and houses, and little almost erased garden plots, the thick growth of Bayberry and Elder offered me all the sticks I needed.

. . . I was so happy trundling home my barrowload of sticks piled to toppling, and finally tipping it up at the garden gate. It took the whole afternoon to stick the Peas and I enjoyed every moment of it. Before putting the dry brittle branches in the ground, with a small light hoe I went all over and through the earth about the Sweet Peas, uprooting Chickweed and Clover, Pigweed and Dog Fennel, till there was not a weed to be seen near them. When night fell I had only just finished this pleasant work.

May 21st: Weeding all day in the hot sun; hard work but pleasant. I find it the best way to lay two boards down near the plot I have to weed and on them spread a waterproof, or piece of carpet, and kneeling or half reclining on this, get my face as close to my work as possible. Sitting flat on these boards, I weed all within my reach then roll up a bit of carpet not bigger than a flat-iron holder, put it at the edge of the space I have cleared, and lean my elbow on it. That gives me another arm's-length that I can reach over. And so I go on till all is done. I move the rest for my elbow here and there as needed among the flowers. It takes me longer to weed than most people because I will do it so thoroughly.

May 23rd: Again hot, still, and splendid. Spent all the morning hammering stakes down into the beds near Hollyhocks, Sunflowers, Larkspurs, Lilies, Roses, single Dahlias, and all the tall growing things. Many were tall enough to fasten to the stakes; all will be, presently. One enormous red Hollyhock grew thirteen feet high by actual measurement before it stopped last year in a corner near the piazza. Oh, but he was superb!

May 24th: Last night after having given myself the pleasure of watering the garden, I could not sleep for anxiety about the slugs. I seldom water the flowers at night because the moisture calls them out and they have an orgy feasting on my most precious children all night long. Before going to bed I went all over the enclosure and, alas, I found them swarming on the Sweet Peas—baby slugs, tiny creatures covering the tender leaves and the dry Pea-sticks, even—thick as grains of sand. I was in despair. And though

I knew they did not mind ashes, I took the fine sifter and covered Peas, sticks, slugs and all, with a thick smothering cloud of wood ashes. Then I left them with many misgivings and went to bed—but not to sleep for thinking of them. At twelve o'clock I said to myself: 'You know the slugs don't care a rap for all the ashes in the world. But the friendly toads may be kept away by them, and who knows if such a smother of them may kill the precious Peas themselves?' I could not bear it any longer, rose up, and donned my dressing gown. And out into the dark and dew I bore the hose over my shoulders coiled, to the very farthest corners of the garden, and washed off every atom of ashes in the black midnight, and came back and slept in peace.

June 3rd: This has been an exciting day, for the Water Lilies I sent for a week ago came in a mysterious damp box across the ocean foam. I had made their tubs all ready for them, putting in the bottom of each the "well-rotted manure" and over this, rich earth and sand mixed in proper proportions. These tubs, or rather large tall butter firkins, stood ready in their places along the sunniest and most sheltered bed in the garden. Oh, the pleasure of opening that box and finding each unfamiliar treasure packed so carefully in wet moss, each folded in oiled paper to keep it moist, and each labeled with its fascinating name. The great pink Lotus of Egypt, the purple Lily of Zanzibar and the red one of the same sort, the golden Chromatella, the pure white African variety and the smaller native white one, the yellow Water Poppy, and the little exquisite plant called Parrot's Feather that creeps all about over the water and has the wonderful living, metallic green of the plumage of the handsome green parrots. These, with the flourishing Water Hyacinth I already had growing in its tub on the steps, and the bright pink Cape Cod Lily, make ten tubs of water plants—a most breathlessly interesting family! And I must not forget another tub of seedling Water Lilies that I am watching with the most intense interest also. It took most of the long, happy day to plant all these in the rich wet mud and settle them in their comfortable quarters. I laid some horseshoes I had picked up at different times (and saved) round the roots to hold them down temporarily while I gently flooded the tubs with water—and rejoiced to see the lovely leaves float out on the surface fresh as if they were at home. Then I sifted clean beach sand over the earth about them to the depth of an inch or more, to hold the soil down and keep the water clear. And all was done. What delight to look forward to the watching and tending of these new friends.

Escholtzia—it is an ugly name for a most lovely flower. California Poppy is much better. Down into the sweet plot I go and gather a few of these, bringing them to my little

table and sitting down before them—the better to admire
and adore their beauty. In the slender green glass in which
I put them they stand clothed in their delicate splendor.
One blossom I take in a loving hand the more closely to
examine it, and it breathes a glory of color into sense and
spirit which is enough to kindle the dullest imagination.
The stems and fine thread-like leaves are smooth and cool
gray-green, as if to temper the fire of the blossoms (which
are smooth also, unlike almost all other Poppies that are
crumpled past endurance in their close green buds) and
make one feel as if they could not wait to break out of the
calyx and loosen their petals to the sun to be soothed into
even tranquillity of beauty by the touches of the air. Every
cool gray-green leaf is tipped with a tiny line of red. Every
flower bud wears a little pale-green pointed cap like an elf.
And in the early morning when the bud is ready to blow, it
pushes off the pretty cap and unfolds all its loveliness to the
sun. Nothing could be more picturesque than this fairy cap,
and nothing more charming than to watch the blossom push
it off and spread its yellow petals slowly rounding to the
perfect cup.

As I hold the flower in my hand and think of trying to
describe it, I realize how poor a creature I am; how impotent
are words in the presence of such perfection. It is held
upright upon a straight and polished stem, its petals curving
upward and outward into the cup of light, pure gold with a

lustrous satin sheen. A rich orange is painted on the gold, drawn in infinitely fine lines to a point in the center of the edge of each petal so that the effect is that of a diamond of flame in a cup of gold. It is not enough that the powdery anthers are orange bordered with gold; they are whirled about the very heart of the flower like a revolving Catherine-wheel of fire. In the center of the anthers is a shining point of warm sea-green, a last consummate touch which makes the beauty of the blossom supreme. Another has the orange suffused through the gold evenly almost to the outer edges of the petals which are left in bright light-yellow with a dazzling effect. Turning the flower and looking at it from the outside, it has no calyx. But the petals spring from a simple pale-green disk, which must needs be edged with sea-shell pink for the glory of God! The fresh splendor of this flower no tongue nor pen nor brush of mortal man can fitly represent.

. . . And here let me say that the secret of keeping Poppies in the house two whole days without fading is this: they must be gathered early before the dew has dried in the morning. I go forth between five and six o'clock to cut them while yet their gray-green leaves are hoary with dew, taking a tall slender pitcher or bottle of water with me into the garden, and as I cut each stem, dropping the flower at once into it so that the stem is covered nearly its whole length with water—and so on till the pitcher is full. Gathered in this way, they have no opportunity to lose their freshness. Indeed, the exquisite creatures hardly know they have been gathered at all.

When I have all I need, I begin on the left end of this bookcase which most felicitously fronts the light, and into the glasses put the radiant blossoms with an infinite enjoyment of the work. The glasses (thirty-two in all) themselves are beautiful. Nearly all are white, clear and pure, with a few pale green and paler rose and delicate blue, one or two of richer pink—all brilliantly clear and filled with absolutely colorless water through which the stems show their slender green lengths. Into the glasses at this end on the left I put first the dazzling white single Poppy, the Bride, to lead the sweet procession—a marvelous blossom whose pure white is half transparent, with its central altar of ineffable green and gold. A few of these first. Then a dozen or more of delicate tissue-paper like blossoms of snow in still another variety (with petals so thin that a bright color behind them shows through their filmy texture). Then the double kind called Snowdrift, which being double makes a deeper body of whiteness flecked with softest shadow. Then, I begin with the palest rose tints, placing them next and slightly mingling a few with the last white one—a rose tint delicate as the palm of a baby's hand. Then the next with a faint suffusion of a blush, and go on to the next shade, still very delicate, not deeper than the soft hue on the lips of the great whelk shells in southern seas. Then, the damask rose color and all tints of tender pink; then the deeper tones to clear rich cherry, and on to glowing crimson—through a mass of this to burning maroon.

To the left of this altar of flowers is a little table, upon which a picture stands and leans against the wall at the back. In the picture two Tea Roses, long since faded, live yet in their exquisite hues, never indeed to die. Before this I keep always a few of the fairest flowers, and call this table—The Shrine.

Near my own seat in a sofa corner at one of the south windows stands yet another small table covered with a snow-white linen, embroidered in silk as white and lustrous as silver. On this are gathered every day all the rarest and loveliest flowers as they blossom that I may touch them, dwell on them, breathe their delightful fragrance and adore them. Here are kept the daintiest and most delicate of the vases which may best set off the flowers' loveliness—the smallest of the collection (for the table is only large enough to hold a few). There is one slender small tumbler of color-less glass from the upper edge of which a crimson stain is diffused halfway down its crystal length. In this I keep one glowing crimson Burgundy Rose, or an opening Jacqueminot bud. The effect is as if the color of the rose ran down and dyed the glass crimson. It is so beautiful an effect. . . .

I love to pore over every blossom that unfolds in the garden, no matter what it may be—to study it and learn it by heart as far as a poor mortal may. If one but gazes closely into a tiny flower of the pale blue Forget-me-not, what a chapter of loveliness is there! One sees at a glance the sweet color of the starry compact cluster, and perhaps will notice that the delicate buds in their cherishing calyx are several shades of rose and lilac before they unclose. But unless one studies it closely, how shall one know that in most cases the *himmel-blau* petals are distinctly heart-shaped, that round its golden center it wears a necklace of pearls? (Or so they seem till on looking closer one discovers that the effect is made by the fluting of the whitened folds of each petal at the base; it looks precisely as if it wore a string of polished beads.) The tiny spot of darkness within its inmost yellow ring holds five stamens with dusty anthers of paler yellow—also heart-shaped when the flower first unfolds—in a close circle round the pistil of pale green. Unless the eyes are young and keen a microscope only will tell this; but it is one of the wisest things in the world to carry in one's pocket a little magnifying glass. For this opens so many unknown gates into the wonders and splendors of Creation.

LETTERS

Preface

Letter writing was the only form of long distance communication until the first telegraph cable was laid across the Atlantic Ocean near the Isles of Shoals in 1866. Celia Thaxter's early letters are addressed to family members and her close friend Lizzie Hoxie at Curzon's Mill in Massachusetts. As newlyweds Celia and Levi had lived on the Curzon property, and after moving to Newtonville Celia exchanged domestic confidences with Lizzie about marriage and children.

The letter excerpts included here are in chronological order and touch on Celia's personal life more than any of her other writing. As the shy islander reached beyond the insularity of the family circle to editors, fans, and literary colleagues, her confidence also expanded. The initial self-effacing tone of a letter to James Fields, influential editor of *The Atlantic Monthly*, with his mentoring quickly gives way to self-assurance. And by 1868 she's discussing the intimate details of a dinner party she attended which the Fields gave in honor of Charles Dickens.

Around this time, Celia engaged in correspondence with an equally famous New Englander, poet John Greenleaf Whittier. While moored on the Shoals, she writes Lizzie that Levi is on a seven-month expedition. In her husband's absence she proposes visiting her friend, with a side trip across the river to see John Whittier. Afterward, she dashes off a brief note telling him what a lovely time she had in Amesbury, adding, "I thank you with all my heart!" An excerpt from a nine-page letter underscores the depth of Celia's devotion to this older man. Despite a later request that their correspondence undergo the silence of fire, several letters to Whittier are included in the LETTERS OF CELIA THAXTER collected by Annie Fields and Rose Lamb. (Houghton Mifflin Co. 1895, 230pp.) Unfortunately, literature and literary writers gave way to mass market publishing, and this book no longer is in print. We owe much to these two friends who recognized the intrinsic value and literary interest of Celia's correspondence. Some of Thaxter's strongest, most poignant writing is to be found in these letters.

During the 1870s, her extraordinarily full life was inscribed by a number of bizarre deaths. Annie Fields, affectionately called Owlet (Celia was Sandpiper), is addressed in many of the letters during this troublesome period. "My imagination will not cease picturing it all," Celia writes of Norwegian friends Anethe and Karen who were brutally slaughtered by an axe murderer on Smutty-Nose Island in 1873. And four years later upon the death of her mother: "It seems as if the whole range of Himalayas lay on my heart." In expressively rich detail she recounts finding their mutual friend, William Hunt, face down in a shallow pool of water behind her Appledore cottage. It is a haunting description.

In 1880 Celia's brother Oscar accompanied her on a voyage to Europe. Like most middle class Americans, she was familiar with the cathedrals, antiquities, and Renaissance paintings portrayed in lithographs and drawings. And for the most part, her descriptions typify those of the innocent abroad. But once she's surrounded by water again, Thaxter sets aside her impressions of the rushed tourist with BAEDECKER in hand.

At Venice where she "went down to the shores of the open Adriatic and picked up shells," the lavish palaces fade away. What really interests Celia are the sleek black gondolas, colorful boatmen, shells, the water. In Marseilles, France, she and Oscar walk along the harbor where "the ships from all lands and climes nearly pitched their cargoes out upon our heads as we threaded our devious way." Celia's prose sparkles when she's gathering flowers and observing people on the Mediterranean.

During an era when everything from the brain to the human palm was mapped for character traits, graphologists might have taken one look at Celia's garlanded centered script and attributed her with benevolence, congeniality, and an upright nature. The content of Celia Thaxter's private correspondence certainly attests to these strengths, and at the same time, reveals the anguish hidden beneath her public persona.

LETTERS

To Elizabeth Curzon Hoxie. Newtonville, Massachusetts, March 28, 1857.

John and Karl have grand times out doors and get dirtier than a whole dictionary can express. I do my own washing now, and think of you all the time, and get tired to death and half dead. But unlike you, I fret and worry when things go wrong, and scold and fuss. Oh, for your patience! How mine takes wing and leaves me forlorn and ugly and horrid. How it seems as if the weary load of things one makes out to do, with such expenditure of strength and nerves and patience, goes for naught—no manner of notice ever taken of all that is accomplished. But if anything is left undone, ah me, the hue and cry that is raised.

To Elizabeth Hoxie. Newtonville, July 10, 1861.

I had such a good time at the island, and when I came home Levi met me in Boston and triumphantly informed me I could go home by land or water, as he had rowed in from Newtonville with George Folsom, and Karl and John, and Henry Weiss. Well, I had started from the island between four and five o' clock and floated on the unruffled bosom of the broad Atlantic until between nine and ten with Lony

[Roland, her son] asleep on my knees, and felt as if I had quite enough water for one day. But I perceived my spouse would particularly like to have me be rowed home, so I embarked at Cambridge bridge, a cushion behind me, an umbrella over me, a box of strawberries in my lap, and four admiring masculine bipeds opposite me.

We had on board two baskets which accompanied me from the island as baggage, champagne baskets containing heaps of beautiful loaves of bread, and six big lumps of fresh butter, a great huge plank of sponge cake, and a huge loaf of plum [cake], a great many corned mackerel, splendid salt fish, and two lovely, indeed I may say heavenly, jars of fresh potted lobster. So we feasted.

At present we subsist principally on ice cream, Levi having invested in a freezer which really and truly freezes in five minutes, and will freeze in four a small quantity. And to tell you the truth, the reason I am writing to you tonight is because I am afraid to go to bed after a big plateful (flavored with strawberries freshly mashed up in it and sherry wine). A jolly mixture, I assure you.

. . . Karl and John do nothing but fight. They live on it all the time. It's their bread and meat and drink. I suppose it's a natural instinct—to prepare them for the war. They roared in chorus, all three under the windows at supper time tonight. And on going out I found Karl and Roland (K. aged nine, R. aged three) beating each other with barrel staves.

Highly agreeable and salutary performance, but disagreeably noisy with company on hand.

To James T. Fields. Newtonville, September 23, 1861.
I thank you very much for the kind things you have said about my little poem, and am grateful for the trouble you took in looking it over and making suggestions. I am sorry I could not act upon them all. I am not good at making alterations. The only merit of my small productions lies in their straightforward simplicity, and when that bloom is rubbed off by the effort to better them, they lose what little good they originally possessed.

I am afraid you will not think the unconscious quotation from the "Ancient Mariner" remedied by the mere transposition of words. But I cannot alter it satisfactorily and say what I wish. If the first and fifth verses do not seem to you too objectionable, pray let them pass. I'm sorry its name is not so felicitous as "Land-Locked," which Mr. Lowell christened.

Pray pardon me for trespassing on your valuable time, and believe me

Gratefully yours,
C. Thaxter

To James Fields. Newtonville, October 25, 1862.
My Dear Friend: I'm sorry I've as yet no prosaic manuscripts

for you, but I pray your patience for a little longer. . . The rhymes in my head are all that keep me alive, I do believe, lifting me in a half unconscious condition over the ashes heap so that I don't half realize how dry and dusty it is! I have had no servant at all for a whole week, by a combination of hideous circumstances. I wish you'd tell A. [Annie Fields] that I have had infinite satisfaction and refreshment out of her tickets already, and forget all weariness and perplexity on the crest of a breaker of earthly bliss while Emerson discourses.

To James Fields. Newtonville, February 20, 1863.
Thanks also for your note of acceptance. Here is the snow again, just as we were fairly rid of the ice-packs. It was so blissful to see the color of the brown fields and pastures, like a tawny lion's skin spread down, and now they are all stark, white, motionless, mute, dead in their shroud again. I hate the snow with a delightful fervor. It just means death to me, and nothing more or less. I sympathize with the cats and hens who step across it, lifting up their feet with intense discomfort and disapprobation, and never walk on it if I can help it. But it won't last long.

To Elizabeth Hoxie. Newtonville, April 24, 1865.
. . . Roland reverently gathered a skunk cabbage flower and carried it up to school in West Newton to the teacher

of botany in whose class he was a pupil and she hove it out of the window with speed. Said she never saw it before and never wished to see it again—Never even heard of it and didn't want to. There's wisdom for you! As if it didn't have its place in creation and wasn't curious and interesting in spite of its smell. Imagine Levi's extreme disgust. A scholar who brought two dabby azalea blossoms from a greenhouse was welcomed with smiles. Such is life.

I tied bones to the trees this winter in humble imitation of you and the birds came round in flocks, to my intense satisfaction.

The boys and Levi have guns and go murdering round the country in the name of science till my heart is broken into shreds. They are horribly learnéd, but that doesn't compensate for one little life destroyed, in my woman's way of viewing it.

To James Fields. Boston, Massachusetts, Monday Morning, January 6, 1867.

Dear Friend: I have copied my ballad for your dissecting knife, very hastily, but I hope it is legible.

Please say to A. [Annie Fields], with much love, that we had a most charming time last night. It was a real delight to see Mr. Dickens [Charles Dickens] and to have one's ideal of an individual so completely realized.

To John Greenleaf Whittier. Shoals, Sunday, February 16, 1868.

Dear Friend, you would hardly know the place! This long piazza, up and down which youth and romance were wont to meander through the summer evenings is filled with snow from one end to the other, and traversed occasionally by the cows and sheep. The little garden which kept me in roses so long last summer, and whose golden and flame-colored flowers seemed trying to outblaze the sun, is but a heap of snow and desolation. How the poppies nodded their scarlet heads between the rails, and how sweet was the perfume from the mignonette, and how good you were to let me put flowers in your buttonhole. Dear me, what a crowd of reminiscences. Not a boat on the moorings where the tiny fleet tossed like eggshells. And the landing where so many tender greetings passed is torn plank from plank and flung to the right and left with a vengeance.

Tuesday, February 18th: We hung the parrot out at the door . . . She likes to be out in the sun, but when she grew tired she called me, "Celia, Celia!" till we took her in. Then she said, "God love that girl!" as she hears Oscar say. How you must miss Charlie. This bird is worth half a dozen people for entertainment. She flew away while mother was gone last autumn, over to Star, and the islanders (taking her for a hawk) were about to shoot her when she called loud and clear, "Cedric!" and just saved herself.

I had a splendid mail today—five letters, some very unexpected epistles, but I did not hear from you therefore I was a little bit disappointed, being a woman and necessary unreasonable. My spouse writes, "Katy [the housekeeper] does bravely and I shall not expect you yet." Isn't he good? Mother says, " A few days longer. You know you'll never have another mother and I shall not be here long." So I linger and linger, but must soon go, sometime next week. I wish I weren't going to set foot off the island till next December! L. [Levi] says he went to a ball unto which we were invited after I came away, the most prodigious affair of the kind ever given in Boston. The flowers alone cost fifteen hundred dollars—with Crete crying out to us, and the freedmen suffering, and the poor children in the streets of Boston barefoot and squalid.

Thursday morning. A really beautiful day. The coast has really got its feet in the water at last. Po Hill [near Whittier] is no longer hanging between heaven and earth like Mohammed's coffin, but has settled down like a decorous hill behind Boar's Head, which stands out like a fort of snow in the morning light. Everything smiles and dances and sings for joy, and oh to be a great gull floating aloft in the pure air!

To Elizabeth [Lizzie] Curzon Hoxie. Appledore, March 7, 1869.

Did you know Karl and I are moored here for seven months? Such is the remarkable fact. And Levi, Lony [Roland, her son] , and John are gone down to Jacksonville, or rather to the state of Florida generally and promiscuously, with powder and shot by the ton, and arsenic and plaster ditto, and camp kettle and frying pan and coffee pot and provisions and rubber blankets and a tent, and a boat, and three guns, and a darkey to be obtained upon arriving at Jacksonville, and heaven only knows what besides. They are to steam down to Enterprise and then take their boat onto the lakes at the end of the St. John's River, and then row back in their boat, shooting all the crocodiles, parakeets, mocking birds, herons, flamingoes, white ibises and every other creature, feathered or otherwise, that chances to fall in their way until they stop in St. Augustine, and then return sometime in May and stop here for awhile to examine the windfall of birds killed by the lighthouse in the spring. And then they are to pursue their way up north to Nova Scotia or the coast of Labrador, still to pursue the unwary sea fowl and cure the skin thereof and bring it as a tribute to the feet of Science.

Meanwhile, Karl and I remain here, moored for seven months. Our house is let and we're houseless and homeless. When the Mayflower is in blossom I purpose skimming across the water and seeking you on one side and friend Whittier on the other side of the broad and meandering Merrimack, and making a flying call on you both.

To John Greenleaf Whittier, 1869.
I wonder if you care to know how the great Beethoven looked? Even if you don't, I think the picture is interesting as a fine type of humanity, and I crave permission to add it to your collection of photographs. . .

I had such a happy time at Amesbury. And I thank you with all my heart!

To Elizabeth Hoxie. Newtonville, January 24, 1870.
Did I tell you John is to live with the Folsoms in Dedham? And Karl and I go to the island—at present at least. Levi means to come home in May, or just as soon as it is warm enough. Then heaven knows where he will go or what we shall do, but something will have to be arranged for next winter. "Come home," I say. There won't be any more home, which makes me feel forlorn.

To Elizabeth Pierce. Isles of Shoals, Wednesday, March 12, 1873.
Today, Dear, I got your sweet little note. Ever so many thanks for it. Lots of newspapers came with such distracted accounts of the murder that it is enough to make anybody

sick. As if a Star Islander did it! If they do not hang that wretch, law is a mockery.

To Feroline Fox. Shoals, November 13, 1873.
Perhaps you don't know that I am a fixture here for the winter. My mother has been so poorly I could not leave her, and she would not leave my brothers. So I must leave my family to take care of themselves and stay with her. For our family is so destitute of women it is really forlorn. No sisters, daughters, aunts, cousins. Nothing but a howling wilderness of me! I would fain unite the duties of existence and have my mother at home with me. But alas, fate has arranged it otherwise, and here we are imprisoned as completely as if we were in the Bastille. A mail perhaps once in a fortnight, and the demoniacal northwest wind mounting guard over us day and night, and howling like ten thousand raving fiends.

I wish you could see the room into which I took you to see my mother. I have taken the plants in hand, and really the desert blossoms like the rose—ten windows full. They are really splendid. A passion flower is running round the top at the rate of seven knots an hour.

To Annie Fields. Shoals, May 20, 1874.
I am full of sadness and of sympathy over this terrible disaster [the Smutty-Nose murder of Karen and Anethe Christensen].

Hardly can I think of anything else, and those two dear people haunt my little room, the sunny piazza, the little garden. I see and hear them everywhere. How gentle they were, how sweet and good and noble.

It is heavenly beautiful here now. Only I am too much alone, and get sadder than death with brooding over this riddle of life. . . I can see how they looked, what they did, what they said; my imagination *will not* cease picturing it all.

To Elizabeth Pierce. Shoals, September 29, 1874.
. . . here in the cottage parlor the fire burns bright; the gas fills the room with light; the rich flowers glow and send out fragrance. My davenport I have wheeled to the fireside. Karl and Miss Parkman are playing bézique close by. The room is so charming. There are thirty-two pictures in it now. I had such a birthday! No end of pictures and things. It was on the 29th of June, and I was smothered with roses. How happy I was. Oh, what a lovely, lovely summer.

I have begun to draw and paint, and find I can do it, even without lessons, with more success, so that I am sure that by and by (after I have had some lessons), I can do it well.

To John Weiss. Shoals, October 17, 1874.
I have been extremely interested in Professor Huxley's address before the British Association, which I have in the *Living Age*. There is nothing so interesting to me as

this quarrying of bright minds, this digging at the roots of things.

No wonder Tyndall took your discourse to bed, but not to sleep. Your note has made this dull day of November warm and bright. Be sure no human creature rejoices in your joy more sincerely, with more loving enthusiasm than your grateful CELIA THAXTER

To Annie Fields. Newtonville, Sunday, November 13, 1876.

Oh, Annie, this morning a brig went ashore on White Island ledge in the fog, at eight o'clock. The breakers tore off her stern and drowned five men there, then tossed the vessel upon Londoners', close by us, and drowned three more. Only one man escaped to tell the tale, and he says he knows not how he saved his life. He found himself on shore, banged and bruised, all his mates gone and the great brig a heap of bristling ruins broken in half high and dry on the iron rocks. There is a little deserted hut on the island, and he made his way to that, found a stove and fuel within, and kindled a fire there. The smoke of this fire was seen soon as the fog lifted.

. . . Part of the vessel's log drifted to our island—a couple of loose pages, and a huge round hoop, one of those which hold a sail to a mast. I cannot describe to you how dreadfully we feel about it so near to us. That one survivor is at Star Island; how he must feel tonight. The leaves of the log-book were records of days last August on a voyage from Annapolis (N.B.) to Barbados. All sorts of things drift ashore. I am afraid of the beaches. Eight men are lying drowned about these remorseless rocks.

To Annie Fields. Appledore, 1877.
Mr. Hunt said to me once, "You are not afraid; therefore you will be able to do anything," and I never forget it. I live in these little landscapes I fashion. I love the flowers and living things and quaint Japanese I work among, with a perfect passion. It [painting] is all my entertainment, all the amusement I have, you know. I am up at six o'clock every morning, often before, laying my plans for dinner for the family of eleven. For since mother has been ill (six weeks now) I have attended to the housekeeping—getting ready the dessert and laying everything in train for the noonday meal—that I may paint every minute of daylight that I can steal.

To Annie Fields. Wednesday night, November 14, 1877.
Dearest Annie, this morning, at half past seven, the sweetest mother in the world went, God alone knows where, away from us. There is no comfort for us anywhere except by the gradual hand of time. The "consolation of religion" I cannot bear. I can bear my anguish better than their emptiness, though I am crushed breathless by my sorrow.

She lies close by me, like a lily flower, her snow-white hair under her snow-white cap of delicate lace, and her sweet hands folded, her pillow strewn with the brightest flowers that blow—scarlet geraniums, gold chrysanthemums, and blood-red roses and bright blush roses. She is white enough to cool their ardent colors, and beautiful she looks.

. . . I never left her a moment this last week; she clung to my hand day and night. We had no stranger. Mina and I did everything ourselves, night and day. This morning, when she died, we did for her all that was necessary, and made her comely and beautiful for her coffin, with only our own hands. She breathed her life away so softly she looks like a dear, quiet child.

It seems as if the whole range of the Himalayas lay upon my heart. Shall I ever breathe freely again, I wonder?

To Annie Fields. Shoals, July 19, 1879.

Just think of our having William Hunt here, just shuddered back from the dreadful verge, so attenuated, so pathetic. He and his sister and his brother, and his man Carter, are all housed beneath this cottage roof, and I hope and trust the air is going to do everything for him.

Everybody is taking care of him, W. H. I mean . . . I told him I wished he would consider my little den, my nook, my bower, this fresh and fragrant little parlor as his own particular property. And he said, "You dear child. You don't know what a miserable, sick, weak, good-for-nothing I am, fit only for my bed." But he really is coming back to life, and eats and sleeps again, and yesterday rowed a little in the children's boat on the pond, and takes an interest in things—in the charming music of the band, etc.

. . . I found him. It was reserved for me, who loved him truly, that bitterness. All the island was seeking him. It was I who went to the brink of that lovely little lake, round which the wild roses have breathed and glowed all summer, and the little birds have come to drink and wash in the early morning light at its peaceful brim.

The lady whose room was behind the parlor said she saw him go up to the reservoir and stand on its stone edge and look into the water, and then toward the house, and then back to the water. At last he came back past the window where I sat painting, and in again, and sat down on the sofa. "Oh, William," I said, "you are quite wet. Don't go out again till it clears off. Stay here by the fire." He stayed a few minutes (he never stays anywhere longer—so restless), and then he went out of the door, and I never saw him again alive.

. . . Up onto that bright, sunny piazza of mine, where he had watched the flowers and heard the music all summer long, they laid his beautiful, dripping length, his gold watch-chain glittering, swinging.

To Annie Fields. Milan, Italy, November 14, 1880.

Oh this place; it is so charming! One eternal and chronic Italian opera all day and all night. Such great basses and tenors superbly sounding through the night. Such flashing dark eyes and midnight hair and men of all sorts and sizes, all wearing long cloaks with one end cast over the shoulder with a grace which is indescribable. And women wearing over the head a square of black lace, one corner gathered over the head, the rest falling over the shoulders and down the back.

. . . Last night we [Celia's eldest brother Oscar accompanied her to Europe] went out soon after we arrived, into the splendid arcade through the square where the colossal statue of Leonardo da Vinci loomed white in the moonlight with the four pupils at the corners of the lofty pedestal. Through the wonderful arcade we passed—it was all glittering with shops and royal stuffs and jewels—and out into the square beyond where the cathedral lifted its forest of white marble spires like frost work, to the moon. Wonderful. Wonderful!

This morning we climbed up and out on its roof in the midst of those exquisite spires each with its statue atop. The city lay half in soft haze below, half revealed—a lovely picture. This afternoon we went to a great performance in the cathedral. The immense interior was filled with a great multitude. There were clouds of incense, and cords of golden crosses and tons of candles flaring. The long procession moved round the church among the people singing, chanting, and organ-playing. I saw a priest the living image of John G. Whittier, and a younger one who looked like my Roland.

. . . Oh, the pathos of it all. Every face a study. Such devotion, such love and sorrow and fearful hope. In all the service in England and everywhere there is but one cry to which my heart responds. It seems the one significant utterance. It is, "Lord have mercy upon us," helpless and defenseless that we are.

Venice, 16th November: Last night in a wonder of white moonlight, we glided into this marvel of the world. Out of the dark railroad station we emerged into the moonlight, on the stone steps where the gondolas were drawn up black against the quay. We were put on board one of these curious charming things and waited while our baggage was hunted up. The cushioned seats were delightful after the rush and jar of the railroad car, the long-continued rattle of the express train.

How delicious it was—the rest and quiet, the balmy air, the salt odors, the sheen of moonlight on the glassy tide, the hundreds of lamps reflected from houses, gondolas, all kinds of craft, the delicious language in which the boatmen talked and called to each other.

. . . We went down to the shores of the open Adriatic and picked up shells; they were delicate and exquisite. We floated in the gondola when we came back up and down the Grand Canal in the sunset, half a mile beyond the Rialto and past such palaces.

. . . Annie, the water is peacock-blue or green the live-long time. And as for the sails, they are color gone mad. Such old gold, and tawny richness of red and orange, and their shapes. Indescribable! The gondolas are the most elegant things; their shape, their uniform black, set off with the glittering brass seahorses or dragons, polished like glass on the gunwale of each side. The carving and brass work on some of them is very rich. And the men who engineer them with such grace and dexterity, so that they glide like magic in the narrowest watery ways, no matter how crowded.

To Annie Fields. Naples, Italy, December 8 , 1880.
We do so rush, I *can't* get the time to write, and I get so tired that it is seldom I can write at five o'clock in the morning as I am doing now.

. . . Our hotel is high up above the smells. Before us lies Capri, melting in sapphire and amethyst. The Mediterranean is wondrous; it is like the Arabian Nights. Tongue can't tell its color—its greens, blues, purples, its lambent light. It's not like water; it's like leaping liquid, prismatic flame all about its delicious islands. Its very substance is colored as if you dripped the fine brilliant blue color we have for washing clothes (you know) into a cup of water. It doesn't owe alone its marvelous effects to reflections from the sky. We see Vesuvius smoking away, the broad red-hot band of lava down its black side. Just this moment it is splendid, its great dark mass heaved high against the crystal-pure sunrise sky. Not a cloud in the whole heaven except the mountain's own long floating plume that trails across the sky from east to west and catches all the faint rose-tints of the coming sun.

. . . Then we came to Rome. The first day of December I gathered violets and I went to the grave of Keats. . . I send you a violet leaf I gathered from that little lonely grave, and a rose leaf from Shelley's not far away.

To James and Annie Fields. Hotel de Normandy, Paris, France, January 18, 1881.
Here we are at last in this frozen Paris where everybody has a red nose.

. . .When we left Nice we spent one day in Cannes, and went over to the Island of St. Marguerite and saw where Marshal Bazaine got over the wall, and the prison of the *Iron Mask*. Much I cared for all that! Down I sat upon a stone near the beach and tried to sketch an old well with an ancient water jar on its broad stone edge, and a wall behind it over which the oranges hung their gold, and beyond, the soft soft sky. Ah *that* sky and *this* sky! There's a difference. The great carmine anemones I found at Cannes, and the rose-colored ones, and the armful of eucalyptus I bought for two sous from a pretty peasant girl sitting on a low wall by the roadside, and the field of peas in blossom—rich, royal purple—common peas (such as we eat) clad like Solomon in all his glory. All along the Riviera we saw fields of them white with bloom. But purple ones, whoever heard of such a thing? Old Cannes was most quaint and charming, new Cannes full of lord-grand-high-nabob English. From there we posted to Marseilles.

. . . The old and new harbors entertained my brother much, and me too. We poked about along them a whole morning. The ships from all lands and climes (packed like sardines side by side with their bow sprits over the one long wharf that edged the border of the tideless sea) nearly pitched their cargoes out upon our heads over their bows as we threaded our devious way beneath. There were peanuts and palm nuts, and beans and coffee and cocoa and grain, and bales of mummy wraps to be made into "shoddy." There was cottonseed, wherewith to adulterate the olive oil.

. . . We left Marseilles for Lyons on Thursday. Half way, we lost the last dear stone-pines and precious olive trees. Soon we saw thin ice and sprinkled snow. And by the time we reached Lyons and the delightful little *Hôtel de l'Univers*. It was bitter, oh, bitter cold.

. . . Did I tell you at Rome of the lady next to me at the *table d'hôte* to whom I talked of Pompeii, saying I wished I could only have stayed there as long as I wanted to? She opened her slightly supercilious English eyes with slow surprise, and with that most peculiar intonation, that slow drawl, that curiously aspirated sort of speech: "How extra-ordinary!" she breathed, "I found it *extremely* dull!"

Did I tell you of the party of Americans from New York traveling with a courier? (We met at Naples, and afterwards at the Capitol at Rome again.) And the lady came up to me and begged me to go with her to look at a certain statue near the entrance, which I did, and beheld a quite unusually developed Diana with bow and quiver, hound at knee, and crescent above brow, complete. "Our courier declares it is a statue of Julius Caesar!" she said. "Now *is* it?" "Well," I said, "if Caesar had a figure like this, being a man, he was a phenomenon!" Then I saw that the pedestal of the statue had an inscription with something about Caesar Imperator on it. But it was so absurd I nearly died of laughter on the spot. The lady's aggrieved expression was too funny—instead of telling the courier to go where the woodbine twineth and using the modicum of brains wherewith a merciful Providence had furnished her.

To John Greenleaf Whittier, Shoals, 1884.
All my life I have wondered at myself, of what my pen

wrote of itself of piety and moral feeling. Now I thank God that in me lay the religious sense ready for awakening, the spiritual perception, the capacity to perceive the truth in the Scriptures.

. . . So, Dear Friend, I am become a most humble and devoted follower of Christ, our Christ, for all races have their own Christs to save and help them, one being especially sent for us, "to call sinners to repentance and not the righteous." I understand it all now, and feel as if all my life I had been looking through a window black with smoke. Suddenly it is cleared and I see a dazzling prospect, a glorious hope. There are two elements which Mohini brings which make clear the scheme of things: one is the law of incarnation, the rebirths upon this earth in which all the Eastern nations believe as a matter of course, and to which our Christ refers in one or two of the gospels. And the other, the law of cause and effect called Karma, the results of lives in the past. When salvation is spoken of, it always means the being saved from further earthly lives, and of reaching God and the supreme of joy, the continual wheel of rebirth and pain and death being the hell, the fire of passions that burns forever, the worm of desires that never die.

. . . I saw lovely Rachel Howland at the women's prison where I went to read to three hundred convicts. We spoke of you and she asked me when I should write, to

Celia Thaxter Selected Writings

remember her to you. She put on my head one of the
Friends' caps, (a real one) which she took off her own head.
The loveliest thing. I wish I could wear it always.

To John Greenleaf Whittier, Shoals, April 11, 1889.
You cannot know what a joy your dear letter is to me. I
have read it again and again. Ah, my dear friend, you speak
so kindly. But who in our time has given so much strength
and refreshment as you have done, not only to your friends
and your country, but to all the world which has been
bettered by your living in it?

Yes, I had a quiet, lovely winter in Portsmouth. I did
more writing than for years and was well and content until
about three weeks ago when I was suddenly very ill, as I
have been twice before for no reason that anybody appears
able to find out except "overwork," the doctors say, in years
past. I say as little about it as possible.

I do not mind the thought of death. It means only fuller
life. But there is a pang in the thought of leaving Karl.

. . . I am wrapped up in measureless content as I sit
on the steps in the sun in my little garden where the freshly
turned earth is odorous of the spring. How I hope you can
come to us this summer! Every year I plant the garden
for your dear eyes, with yellow flowers. I never forget
those lovely summers long ago when you came and loved
my flowers.

I am going to send you with this a little copy of an old picture of Karl and myself when we were babes together—he one year old, I eighteen.

Thank you for the beautiful poem you enclosed. It is most lovely. You ask what I have been writing? A great deal—for me. I wish I had sent you the April *St. Nicholas*, for it is a version I made of Tolstoy's "Where love is, there is God also." I had such reverence for the great author's work I hardly dared touch it. But I did it with the greatest love. I called it "The Heavenly Guest." Dear Sarah Jewett has a sweet story begun in the April number, and my poem follows.

Ever with deep, gentle, grateful love,

Your C. T.

To Rose Lamb. Shoals, September 4, 1889.
. . . How curious the thought of the past is. Nearly forty years ago this month I was married. The moonlight on the water looked exactly the same that evening as it does now. How many lives we seem to live in one. I heard the cricket in the grass, the same sound I heard tonight.

To Adaline Hepworth. 47 State St., Portsmouth, New Hampshire, April 8, 1890.
. . . I should have written before, Dear Ada, for I have thought of you much and often. But I have been fighting with nervous prostration all winter, with the waves going

over me until I was well nigh drowned. I have given my strength all away all my life, and now I am bankrupt. But I am fighting my way up out of the N.P. [Nervous Prostration] with the help of a wise old doctor who lives not far from here, who feeds me on champagne, which makes of me a new creature quite. But I've not much strength to write, though I have *so much* to talk about. Do come to the Shoals for as long as you can.

To Adaline Hepworth. Shoals, June 8, 1890.
Yes, indeed, I have been terribly ill—at death's door. Neuralgia of the stomach, the doctor says; too near the heart, you know. It would not yield to morphine or anything (this last attack), and I should have been glad to die except for the thought of Karl. I don't mind the change of state any more than changing the town I live in here, though I don't think anyone gets more enjoyment out of life than I do or loves more God's expression of himself in this world. But I don't shrink in the least at the thought of the change. If Karl could only go with me; he will be so desolate.

To C. E. L. Wingate. Portsmouth, November 22, 1891.
It is a difficult task to choose among Mr. Whittier's poems those which I like best. There are so many that have become a part of my life, so many that appeal with resistless force to every thoughtful soul.

.   .   . Our other famous poets are stars of the same
magnitude, doubtless, but of a different color. And the high
pure light of Whittier's genius burns clear and stands alone
with an immortal beauty of its own, belonging to the things
which are eternal. He is a power for good in his own land
and in the world, a landmark up to which all struggling
souls may look and gather fresh courage to climb. How
many instances I recall in which I have seen his beautiful
words comforting the weariness of age and inspiring with
noble impulses the fiery heart of youth. Truly, I know of no
one who has been more revered and beloved. His very
name is a symbol of truth and unflinching integrity. And the
good he has done comes back to him now in the blessing his
friends and his country bring to him with the homage of
their admiration.

To Sarah Orne Jewett. Portsmouth, 1893.
Thank you for your sweet letter and all your kind suggestions. I had already begun to "reef" my Ms. [probably the
manuscript *An Island Garden*] and perceived at once when
I read it aloud that it must be cut ever so much in places.
Dear, you have given me a real helpful lift, because I have
been doing this work without a particle of enthusiasm in a
most perfunctory manner from the bits of notes I had made.
And my mind has been so saddened by deep shadows for
many months, somehow I had no heart in it at all. I am

hoping when I go to the Shoals presently to get some of the real flavor of the place and the work into it. It doesn't satisfy me one bit. I began to write the introductory chapter right off, and shall I send it to you as you said? I am *so* glad for every bit of criticism. I was so happy when I wrote the Shoals book; it wrote itself. I seemed to have very little to do with it, anyway. But now the shadows are so long, and it grows so lonesome on this earth, and there is such a chill where there used to be such warmth and bliss.

To Feroline W. Fox. Shoals, July 1, 1893.

. . . Karl is with me. My two youngest sons are in Kittery [Maine]. Roland and his dear little family moved down there in the first week of June for the summer. Since he has had a professorship in Harvard, he has such long vacations that I cannot be grateful enough.

The two grandchildren, little Eliot and Katherine, are fascinating to their grandmother. Indeed, I don't think I ever realized what "fun" was until I became a grandmother. Isn't it delightful?

I went over to see them the other day and as Eliot and I were walking together and gathering wild strawberries, with the grass and daisies and buttercups higher than the little fellow's head, he said to me suddenly apropos of nothing at all, "Are you very old, Granna?" "Yes, Dear," I said, "I am very old." He heaved a deep sigh and said, "I am very sorry." "But why, Dear?" I asked. "Because," he said, "I don't want you to be deaded before I am!" He is only four years old and troubling himself so much.

I am pegging away hard on the book and I want to ask you lots of things. All you say is so precious, Dear. I have got a little plan of the garden as you suggested with places of everything marked—a sort of little map. I have got the whole thing about done, the writing, but there is much copying and arranging of parts to make a proper unity. I have been so ill since the house closed, just about *dead* with the stress and bother of things and people, and feared to slip back to the hateful state of three years ago.

To Olive Thorne Miller. Appledore, Isles of Shoals, May 27, 1894.

Your letter just comes and is a great happiness to me . . .

I must tell you that I have devoured every printed word of yours since the first time I discovered you with the most entire sympathy and loving appreciation. I was perfectly delighted last year to find in one of your *Atlantic* papers a quotation from some verses of mine: *Like a living jewel he sits and sings.* Do you remember using it? I was so proud, I wrote to Bradford Torrey about it asking him if he had the happiness of knowing you. I am interested in all you have to say, and how I do wish I knew a fraction of what you do of the birds I love so much.

. . . I am glad you found my book worthy [*An Island Garden*]. We must adore these things, our birds and our flowers, all these manifestations of Divine beauty—if we see them at all, don't you think so?. . . I thank you so much for this dear letter of yours. I treasure it among my most precious things. Truly I have an enthusiasm for *you*, and I'm an old woman, almost sixty. And enthusiasm at sixty means more than it does at sixteen—after one has been banged about through this strange and perplexing life of ours so many years. I wish I could see you.

With thanks and thanks, and a love that has always been yours,

I am yours most truly,
Celia Thaxter

STORIES

Preface

Celia was fifteen when she wrote her first story at Mt. Washington Female Seminary in Boston, and in a letter she mentions that she showed it to her father, who didn't give her much encouragement. Sometime after her first verses were published in *The Atlantic Monthly,* other poems were featured in *Youth's Companion* and *St. Nicholas*, an upscale children's magazine which also included Louisa May Alcott among its list of contributors. Not until Celia was thirty-two did she write more stories.

A letter to *Our Young Folks* displays an uncharacteristic temerity and reserve: "I have many little stories to tell of birds and beasts, and if you like I will send them." Author and social reformer Lucy Larcom was the co-editor of *Our Young Folks* and not only accepted Thaxter's stories but introduced her work to other editors. In effect, the steady commissions from these children's magazines constituted a much needed source of income in the Thaxter household.

Over the years Celia put aside ten of these stories and scores of verses for an anthology but did not complete their arrangement prior to her death. In a prefatory note to STORIES AND POEMS FOR CHILDREN (Houghton Mifflin, 1895), Celia's close friend Sarah Orne Jewett underscores Thaxter's "gift of teaching young eyes to see the flowers and birds; to know her island of Appledore and its sea and sky."

Tiny tots in Victorian New England were clothed like miniature adults and expected to mimic (if not understand) the rigid moral codes of their parents. So a good children's story relied heavily on a string of moral injunctions throughout, with a "lesson" at the end.

But what we learn from Celia's stories is far from the standard McGuffy's platitudes of the era. As with most of Celia Thaxter's writing, the natural environment plays a key role, and in these stories animal instinct supersedes that of human nature.

For instance, after reading "Bergetta's Misfortunes," the child who has never seen a lobster probably will be able to draw one. "The Bear At Appledore" shows children that wild animals do best in their native habitats and won't survive in captivity. Dictums and decorum such as children should be seen and not heard are ignored by Thaxter. Instead, in the story "Almost A Tragedy" she asks young readers to take a hard look at their dinner plates and think about the animals that have been slaughtered to nourish them.

Most of the stories, according to Celia, "hardly are stories at all," but real-life incidents that occurred on the Isles of Shoals. Many of them are amusing and display a light-hearted charm that must have dazzled the imaginations of those proper little boys and girls.

Although the names have been changed, one suspects Celia knew the cast of characters well. Sylvia (Syl) and her two brothers in "Almost A Tragedy" most probably are Celia (Cel) and her own brothers.

Of this group of four stories a fairy tale, "The Spray Sprite," comes closest to genuine fiction. For half a dozen pages Celia clings to a true-to-life description of Appledore before launching her memorable fairy fleet of great purple mussel-shells. Unfortunately, toward the end of this enchanting tale, the heroine suddenly is struck by a strong case of the American work ethic. Unconvincingly, she urges other children to abandon the dream and "get used to the tame life." And so the fairy fleet ebbs away, leaving a high tide of patchwork. One suspects the story has been doctored to please a magazine editor—for moralistic stories of this nature were popular. In light of Celia's early marriage and subsequent hardships, this conventional ending lends a note of sadness to an otherwise joyous creation.

CONTENTS

BERGETTA'S MISFORTUNES

OLD BERGETTA LAY ASLEEP on the doorstep in the sun. Bergetta was a cat of an inquiring mind. Now an inquiring mind is a very good thing if it is not too largely developed; but Bergetta's was of so lively a nature that she was continually led into difficulties thereby. This morning she was having a beautiful nap in the spring sunshine. Her two little white forepaws were gathered in under her chin and she had encircled herself with her tail in the most compact and comfortable way. Now and then she lifted her sleepy lids and winked a little. And perhaps she saw (or did not see) the bright blue ocean at the end of the rocky slope before her and the outline of Appledore Island across the strip of sparkling water and the white sails here and there and the white clouds dreaming in the fresh and tender sky of spring.

It was very pleasant. Bergetta at least enjoyed the warmth and quiet. Her three companion cats were all out of her way at that moment. She forgot their existence. She was only conscious of the kindly rays that sank into her soft fur and made her so very sleepy and comfortable.

Presently, a sound broke the stillness, very slight and far off, but she heard it and pricked up her pretty pink-lined

231

ears and listened intently. Two men bearing a large basket between them came in sight approaching the house from the beach. The basket seemed heavy. The men each held a handle of it and very silently went with it round to the back entrance of the house.

Bergetta settled her head once more upon her folded paws and tried to go to sleep again. But the thought of the basket prevented: *What could be inside that basket?*

She got up, stretched herself, and lightly and noiselessly made her way round the house to the back door and went in. The basket stood in the middle of the floor and the three other cats sat at a respectful distance from it near each other, surveying it doubtfully.

Bergetta wasn't afraid. She went slowly towards it to investigate its contents. But when quite close to it, she became aware of a curious noise going on inside of it—a rustling, crunching, dull, clashing sound which was as peculiar as alarming. She stopped and listened. All the other cats listened. Suddenly a queer object thrust itself up over the edge and a most extraordinary shape began to rise gradually into sight.

Two long, dark, slender feelers waved about aimlessly in the air for a moment. Two clumsy claws grasped the rim of the basket. And by their help a hideous dark bottle-green-colored body patched with vermilion, bristling with points and knobs, and cased in hard, strong, jointed armor with eight legs flying in all directions, each fringed at the foot with short yellowish hair and with the inner edges of the huge misshapen claws lined with a row of sharp, uneven teeth opening and shutting with the grasp of a vise—this ugly body rose into view before the eyes of the astonished cats.

It was a living lobster.

Dear children, those among you who never have seen a living lobster would be quite as astonished as the cats were at its unpleasant aspect. When you see these shell fish they have been boiled and are bright scarlet all over and you think them queer and grotesque—perhaps they do not seem frightful. But a living lobster is best described by the use of the much abused word *horrid*. It seems a mixture of spider and dragon. Its jet-black shining eyes are set on short stalks and project from its head and the round opaque balls turn about on their stems and survey the world with a hideous stolidity. It has a long jointed tail which it clasps together with a loud clash and with which it contrives to draw itself backward with wonderful rapidity.

Such was the hard and horny monster that raised itself out of the basket and fell with a loud noise all in a heap on the floor before Bergetta. She drew back in alarm and then sat down at a safe distance to observe this strange creature. The other cats also sat down to watch, farther off than Bergetta, but quite as much interested.

For a long time all was still. The lobster, probably rather shocked by its fall, lay just where it had landed. Inside the basket a faint stirring and wrestling and clashing was heard from the other lobsters—that was all. Very soon Bergetta felt herself becoming extremely bored with this state of things. She crept a little nearer the basket.

I needn't be afraid of that thing, thought she. It doesn't move anymore.

Nearer and nearer she crept, the other cats watching her but not stirring. At last she reached the lobster that in its wrath and discomfort sat blowing a cloud of rainbow bubbles from its mouth, but making no other movement. Bergetta ventured to put out her paw and touch its hard shell. It took no notice of this, though it saw Bergetta with its queer eyes on stilts, which it wheeled about on all sides to 'view the prospect o'er.'

She tried another little pat. Whereat, the lobster waved its long antennae (or feelers) that streamed away over its back in the air far beyond its tail.

That was charming. Bergetta was delighted. The monster was really playful! She gave him another little pat with her soft paw and then coquettishly boxed his ears—or the place where his ears ought to be. There was a boding movement of the curious shelly machinery about his mouth, an intricate network all covered with the prismatic bubbles he had blown in his wrath. But he was yet too indifferent to mind anything much.

Bergetta continued to tease him. This *was* fun. First with the right and then with the left paw she gave him little cuffs and pushes and pats which moved him no more than a rock. At last he seemed to become suddenly aware that he was being treated with somewhat more familiarity than was agreeable from an entire stranger and began to move his ponderous front claws uneasily.

Still Bergetta continued to frisk about him till he thrust out his eight smaller claws with a gesture of displeasure and opened and shut the clumsy teeth of the larger ones in a way that was quite dreadful to behold.

This is *very* funny, thought Bergetta. I wonder what it means? And she pushed her little white paw directly between the teeth of the larger claw which was opening and shutting slowly. Instantly the two sides snapped together with a tremendous grip and Bergetta uttered a scream of pain. Her paw was caught as in a vise and cut nearly through with the uneven toothed edge.

Alas, alas! Here was a situation. In vain she tried to get away. The lobster's claw clasped her delicate paw in a grasp altogether too close for comfort. Crying with fear and distress, Bergetta danced about all over the room, and everywhere Bergetta danced the lobster was sure to go too, clinging for dear life. Up and down, over and across they went in the wildest kind of jig, while all the other cats made themselves as small as they could in the remotest corners and watched the performance with mingled awe and consternation. Such a noise—Bergetta crying and the lobster clattering, and the two cutting such capers together!

At last someone heard the noise and, coming to the rescue, thrust a stick between the clumsy teeth and loosened the grip of the merciless claw. And poor Bergetta, set at liberty, limped off to console herself as best she might.

For days she went limping about so lame she could hardly creep round the house. When at last she began to feel a little better, she strayed one day into the same room and seeing what she rightly guessed to be a pan of milk on the table, jumped first into a chair and then up on the table to investigate. Naughty Bergetta! Yes. The pan was full of milk not yet skimmed. How luscious. She did not wait for anybody's permission but straightway thrust her pink nose into the smooth, creamy surface.

Now it was washing day and just under the edge of the table behind Bergetta on the floor, a tub full of hot suds had been left. She lifted up her head after her first taste of the cream. How nice it was. Oh, horror! What did she see? Just opposite her on the table was another lobster with its long feelers bristling. It had been boiled, by the way, but of course Bergetta could not know this tranquilizing fact.

Bright scarlet with its dull dark eyes pointed straight at her, it dawned upon Bergetta's terrified vision.

So eager she had been to look into the milk pan, she had not discovered the lobster before, and now her fright was so great that she gave one leap backwards and fell splash into the tub of warm suds.

Good heavens, what a commotion. With eyes, ears, nose, and mouth full of soapy foam, she crawled out of it and more dead than alive, ran to the door and forth into the cold, leaving a long stream of suds on the floor in her wake. The wind blew through her soaked fur and chilled the marrow of her bones.

Poor Bergetta. All the other cats came round her and stared at her with astonishment. And I'm afraid if cats ever do laugh, they certainly laughed at Bergetta when she told them her morning's experience.

I don't think she ever coquetted with a lobster again or tried to steal milk from the pan, but went mewing about, rubbing her cheek against the kind little cook's foot till she gave her all a cat would wish.

And let us hope Bergetta escaped any more such dire disaster during the rest of her life.

THE SPRAY SPRITE

ONCE UPON A TIME, a thousand years ago there dwelt by the sea a little maid. Had I said in the sea it would perhaps have been as well, for such a spray sprite never danced before at a breaker's edge. It was bliss to her to watch that great sea, to hear its sweet or awful voices, to feel the salt wind lift her thick brown hair and kiss her cheek, to wade bare-footed into the singing, sparkling brine.

Above all things, she hated to sew patchwork. Oh, but she was a naughty child—not at all like the good, decorous little girls who will perhaps read this story. She didn't like to sweep and dust and keep all things bright and tidy. She wished to splash in the water the whole day long, and dance and sing, and string shells, and be idle like the lovely white kittiwakes that flew to and fro above her and came at the beckoning of her hand. She looked with scorn on dolls and all their appointments and never wished to play with them. It was almost as bad as patchwork!

But she loved the sky and all the clouds and stars, the sun that made a glory in the east and west at morning and evening, the changing moon, the streaming Northern Lights. The winds seemed human, so much they had to say to her. She thought: the north wind fights me; the west wind plays with me; the east wind sighs and is always ready to weep; the south wind loves and kisses me. Every wave that whitened the face of the vast sea was dear to her. Every bird that floated over, every sail that glided across—all brought her a thrill of joy. And what a wild and keen delight came to her with the thunder, lightning, and the rain.

But with all her heart she hated the cold white snow. Much she liked to creep out of the house in the dusk of dawn and climb the highest rocks to see the morning break. Wrapping herself close from the chill wind, curling into a niche of the rough granite cliff, how beautiful it was all alone with the soaring gulls, to watch the east grow rosy, rosier to the very zenith, till she shouted with joy facing the uprisen sun. Then it was so splendid to stand on the rocks when the billows came tumbling in sending the spray flying high in the air and throwing handfuls of crimson dulse at her, or long brown tresses of seaweed which she caught and flung back again while she was drenched with the shower and the wind blew her about in rough play. And blissful it was to run with the sandpipers along the edge of the shallow waves on the little beach and dance in the clear green water, or at low tide to hang over the still surface of pools among the rocks wherein lay treasures untold.

Oh, those gardens of the sea! Who shall describe their beauty? It was as if a piece of rainbow had fallen and melted into them, such myriads of many-colored creatures and plants inhabited them. Dear children, if I were to talk to you the whole day, I could not tell you half the wonderful things she saw in those clear depths. But I think she liked best of them all the dainty Eolis, a delicate shell-less snail with rosy spines and tiny horns.

To watch all this marvelous life at the edge of the wild ocean was enchanting, and she never wearied of it. Then, among the higher rocks grew a few land plants and grasses and a single root of fern—a world of delight to her. A whole tropical forest would not have been so precious. She gathered plumes of the bright goldenrod that nodded in the clefts, and crowned herself with long garlands of the wild pink morning-glory. And the gulls and the sandpipers looked at her and wondered, I dare say, what she did it for. They could have told quite as well as she. To the little pimpernel always ready to shut its scarlet flowers at the slightest shadow of a cloud, she said, "I love you, pimpernel, for you're always dreaming and that's what I like to do." And so she did dream. And with the everlasting sound of the sea in her ears, I wonder she ever believed anything to be real.

She was a very happy little maid and perfectly content, but still she could not help longing to know what lay beyond the round horizon that hemmed her in with the waves. And many and many a day, rocking in her little boat on the tranquil water, she gazed at the dim line where the sky seemed to rest on the sea and pondered until she was lost in a maze of aimless thought.

"Over there beyond the faint blue cloud of distant coast lies the great world," she said. "Is it beautiful there?" Sometimes at sunrise it looked most beautiful, flushed with delicious color—purple and rose and gold. Vessels glided by hither and thither at all times of the day and night. Whence came they? Whither did they go? If, in the morning sunshine she saw the shadow of one sail fall upon another as some craft passed near, the sight made this little savage so happy that it was better than if she had found a mine of gold—foolish thing to be happy at a shadow.

She laughed and talked with the loons and learned to imitate their weird wild cry. She stretched her arms up to the big burgomaster gull flying over, crying, "Take me to ride with you, burgomaster, between your broad wings!" Driftwood came sailing to the shore, bits of bark. On what tree did they grow, she wondered. Pieces of oars—who had paddled with them? Laths, sticks, straws, blocks, logs, branches, cones tangled with ribbon-grass, kelp and rock-weed—each thing had a history if she did but know it, she thought. Sometimes came a green fir bough. There was a wonder, for no trees grew among her rocks, there was not soil enough to hold their roots. Sometimes she came upon tokens of wreck and disaster that made her heart shrink, for she did not like to think that pain was in this lovely world wherein she was so glad to be alive.

But she always fancied she should find some strange and costly thing as she sought among the weeds and drift— that some mysterious and beautiful thing would come floating across the sea for her among the odds and ends one day. And something did come as you shall hear.

One night she was playing on the beach alone. She gathered shells and seaweeds. Full of joy, she laughed and sang to herself. It was high tide and sunset; all the west was red and clear. A golden glory lay along the calm water from the sinking sun to her feet as she stood at the edge of the tide. Nearby, the lighthouse began to twinkle in crimson and gold. Far off, large vessels with their sails full of the twilight passed by, silent and slow. The waves made a continual talking among themselves, and sweet and disconsolate came the cry of the sandpipers along the shore. All else was very still. She stopped her play and sat down on a rock and let her bare feet drop within reach of the water while she watched the gulls slowly floating home by twos and threes through the lovely evening sky. She smiled to see them beat the air with their wide wings with a slow and measured motion. She knew where their lonesome rock lay, far out on the eastern sea.

By and by all were gone. The red faded, but a pure and peaceful light still held the west, and the stars came out one after one. She sat still there a long time. The warm wind wrapped her close. She felt no chill with the falling dew. Wistfully peering out toward the horizon-line she did not for some time notice that the sea was full of cool fire— sparks that snap and burst and flee. Every wave left its outline in vanishing gold on the wet weeds and sand. Her feet were covered; it was as if she had on golden-spangled slippers. That was charming.

The tide had begun to fall now and left bare a gray rock worn and polished by the waves—heaven knows how many thousands of years—till it was as smooth as satin. She laid her cheek against the dear old gray rock. It was her pet pillow. Though the water had just flowed over the rock, it was warm yet from the sun which had blazed down all the long clear summer day. Then she watched the pale flame glowing and fading, and glowing again, till. . . Well, I never could be quite sure how much of what I am going to tell you she dreamed, and how much really happened, but the main points are certainly true.

After she had been watching and listening awhile, she became aware of an unaccustomed sound among the noises of the washing tide and whispers of the wind. Presently, she perceived between the tidemark and the ebbing water two dim slender figures busy among the weeds, and sweet, clear voices reached her with a merry mingling of talk and laughter. The figures drew near—a youth, dark and brilliant, a maiden, bright and fair. They were filling little baskets with the phosphorescent sparks, and every spark they touched became a permanent star, so that the little baskets were overflowing with the harmless flame. She could not comprehend their talk but she watched them eagerly. The youth dipped his finger into the pale fire and touched with it the girl's white forehead and left there a spark that flickered upward, then brightened and stood steady—a glittering star so beautiful above her dusky hair. And the child saw the fairy maiden blush as she swung the basket lightly to her shoulder. She rose up as they turned and confronted them, and both sprang toward her.

"Child of the spray," they cried, "it is thyself we came to seek." And grasping her hands, they drew her gently after them into a small lonely cove where the water lay like a mirror with all the stars in heaven shining out of it.

And by the starlight what an enchanting sight she saw. Moored close to the beach, a fairy fleet was waiting motionless—seven great purple mussel-shells as large as her own little skiff, each lined with mother-of-pearl and strewn with silken cushions. In each was a tapering mast from which drooped lightly down the idle sail shining like silver, bright as if woven of thistledown. And at each curling prow was set a cluster of phosphorescent stars gleaming and never disappearing, and every boat had its merry crew of fairy creatures. And in the midst alone in his skiff, sat a fairy prince with a golden crown. When they saw their comrades bringing the spray child, they set up a sweet outcry and pushed the boats ashore with slender oars, and leaped out and danced about her.

Was she awake or asleep? The tide had fallen farther yet. A large purple starfish glided on the sand and paused close by. Many-hued little shells crept near and listened, and pearly Eolis from a crystal pool at hand, lifted her crested head to listen also. The child rubbed her eyes and looked about on every side. The sand was real beneath her feet. The familiar sound of the water was surely in her ears. There were the stars above burning steadily. She was awake, she thought, though it was night. But when she looked at the fairy prince, she thought it was sunrise suddenly. He came near and took her hand, and as he did so all the sandpipers cried aloud in their dreams, and made their playmate tremble with mournful foreboding.

"Come," he said. "I have sailed across the sea to show you what lies beyond the wonderful horizon. Come with me."

And without knowing how, she was sitting in the beautiful boat by his side and all the fairy creatures were busy casting off the ropes and trimming the sails with song and shout. And as swiftly those shimmering sails ran up to the tops of the delicate masts, the south wind filled them. Sudden wafts of music fine and sweet rose and fell, and out of the little cove swept the fleet of shells, rustling canvas, gleaming

245

stars, and brilliant faces and all. Rapidly they passed from sight, and then on the lonely beach the sandpipers cried more disconsolately and the waves broke ever with a lonelier sound. For nevermore came that little spraysprite back to play with them again.

What became of her? Well, that I will tell you also. At first, she was listening to such a wonderful story that she quite forgot everything else. But as they sailed and sailed, one by one the fairy crews disappeared. And still little *Idleness* and the fairy prince sailed on and on till at last they came to the great world which had looked so beautiful to the child's eyes from afar—all gold and pearl and rose color.

And of what do you think she found it was made after all? Why, my dear children, only patchwork! Everybody was doing patchwork of one kind or another—black patches and white, blue patches and gray—and everybody was so busy that it was astonishing to witness. I do not mean to say that everybody was sewing with needle and thread, but all were at work upon something. And she comprehended that while she had been dancing in the spray, wiser children had been learning all kinds of useful things of which she knew nothing at all, and how much time she had lost.

At first it was wearisome enough—like living in a big ant-hill with all the ants rushing about pell-mell. And then all the trees, hills, and fields seemed to be crowding up to the windows for the express purpose of smothering the poor mermaid. There wasn't half enough sky and no water at all to speak of, and everything was so stiff and still, except the hurrying people. The trees waved, but they couldn't go sweeping off as the grand ships did over the sea. And as for the fields, they were well enough, but altogether too still. They never changed about like the shifting, musical, many-colored sea. And yet some of them were lovely when the wind bowed all the tall white daisies toward her like the crest of a breaking wave—better so than when they blushed with clover bloom or flamed in buttercups and dandelions. The brooks and rivers were good as far as they went, but there was so little of them. And if she liked the hills, it was because they seemed to her like huge, petrified waves, heaved solemnly against the sky. Alas for her great horizon! She pined for it night and day.

But gradually she began to get used to the tame life. And slowly, very slowly, she found out a secret worth all the beauty she had lost. As young people don't know it gener-ally, I'll whisper it in your ear. This is it: that work is among the best blessings God gave the world; that to be useful and helpful even in the smallest ways brings a better bliss than all the delightful things you can think of put together. And this bliss is within the reach of every human being. She was glad when she found it out for herself.

And so now she does patchwork to the end of her days. Patchwork in this case meaning all kinds of work under the

247

sun, a little here and a little there. You would never know now that she had been a spray sprite and danced among the breakers and talked and laughed with the loons. For she is like everybody else, except that sleeping or waking, year after year she keeps in her ears the sad, mysterious murmur of the sea—just like a hollow shell.

THE BEAR AT APPLEDORE

MR. BRET HARTE ONCE told so charming a story about a bear, dear children, that I hesitate about giving you mine—which, indeed, is hardly a story at all. But perhaps you may like to hear what I have to tell.

Our bear came from Georgia when he was a tiny baby bear. But he was not nice and soft and silky like Mr. Harte's bear—he was rusty and brown and shaggy and rough. And he looked askance at everybody out of his little eyes that were as black as beads. I dare say he did not find it at all agreeable to come all the way from Georgia to the Isles of Shoals. And I am sure he did not find it pleasant after he arrived at his destination.

He was tethered to a stick in a grassy space in front of the house and the children played with him morning, noon, and eve, one whole long summer. Alas, I fear he was often weary of his brief life, and would have been glad never to have been born. For I am sorry to say there were many naughty and thoughtless children among those who played with him—unkind boys who poked at him with sticks and rolled him over and over in his helplessness and teased and tormented him till it was almost too much to be borne. The little girls were kinder. One especially I remember who used to hold him in her arms as if he had been a big kitten and lay his dusky head on her shoulder and put her cheek down against his shaggy crown so tenderly and sit rocking to and fro on the grass with him hours at a time. And often after she went to bed at night I would hear her sighing out of the fullness of her heart, "Oh, that dear, dear bear."

Well, the poor little creature endured his captivity till the eighth day of September when there came a tremendous storm with a wind from the south, which was neither more nor less than a hurricane. Windows were blown in, buildings blown down, shingles ripped off roofs in flying flocks. There was a fine tempest. A great copper-colored arch spanned the black sky at eight o'clock in the evening. The sea lifted itself up and flung itself white with fury all over the island. And in the midst of the tumult the little bear disappeared. Nobody thought of him—there was such a confusion, everybody trying to save themselves from the fearful wind that had smashed the windows and broken into the houses and was destroying everything in spite of all we could do. Terror probably gave the baby bear strength. He tugged wildly at his chain. It broke and he fled away through the dark. And when the morning came we could not find him anywhere.

Fortunately, the gale only lasted a few hours, and at sunrise next day the sea was calm except just about the rocks where it rolled in tremendous breakers and cast clouds of diamond drops up toward the sky. A fishing schooner had been wrecked at the south side of the island. I went over to look at her. It was not cheerful to see her crushed hull heaving helplessly up and down and the poor fishermen sadly picking up, here and there, fragments of ropes, rigging, and fishing gear which the awful sea had spared them. So I wandered away along the shore, and at last sat down on the edge of a high cliff and admired the great, gleaming, sparkling floor of the ocean and the wonderful billows that shattered themselves in splendor between me and the sun. I pushed with my foot a bit of stone over the brink of the crag and heard it fall below. But at the same time I heard another and quite an unexpected sound—a noise hardly to be described— something between a hiss and a whistle, which came up to me from the gorge below. I knew at once it could be nothing but the bear and leaned over and looked down.

Sure enough, there he was, a black heap curled up on a shelf of rock just below me a few feet out of reach. He looked so comfortable, for it was the sunniest, cosiest nook. And little vines of scarlet pimpernel trailed about him, and plumes of goldenrod waved out of clefts in the rock, and a tall mullein stood up still and straight beside him, its head heavy with thick-set seed vessels. I was surprised to see him and very glad, as you may imagine. So I called out in the most engaging tones, "Good morning, my dear. I'm very glad to see you!"

I am pained to say he looked up at me with an expression of intense cunning and unlimited defiance and uttered again that shrill, suspicious, half hiss, half whistle, which being interpreted might signify, "Malediction!"

So fierce he looked and savage, with that distrustful side-long leer out of his black eyes, he was far from being an agreeable object to look at. And as I could not carry him home alone, or even capture him, I was obliged to leave him alone in his glory. But I made a little speech to him over the cliff edge before going away, in which I sympathized with his sorrowful state: If I only could have had you for my own, poor little bear, you should not have been teased and plagued and had your temper spoiled. Don't cherish resentment against me, I beg of you. If you'll only stay here till I come back, I'll bring you something to eat, and lumps of sugar, my dear.

And so I went away and left him snarling. But when I went back he had disappeared, and though we sought for him everywhere, we did not see him again for nearly seven months. I was sure he was alive all the time, snugly stowed away in some deep crevice sucking his paws perhaps, which I had been told was a favorite pursuit of bears in the winter season. But my belief was scorned and flouted by the rest of the family. "What!" they cried. "You think that little creature could live in this zero weather so many weeks, so many months, with nothing to eat? Of course he is frozen to death long ago."

But I believed him to be alive all the same. And I was not surprised when, one evening in April while the sky was warm and crimson with sunset, there rose a cry outside the house, "The bear! The bear!" And from the window I saw him grown twice as large as he had been in the autumn, clumsily climbing over a stone wall nearby. All the men about the house gave chase. But he plunged bravely over the rocks and suddenly disappeared, as a drop of water soaks into the ground in a large seam in the side of the hill. There they found his cave all strewn with bones and the feathers of fowls. They could not dislodge him that night, but in the morning they made a business of it and at last brought him down to the house with a rope around his neck, a most reluctant and indignant quadruped.

As there were no children then to tease him, he led a peaceful life for two months, and I tried by the most persevering kindness and attention to make his days less unhappy. I led him about from place to place, selecting new spots in which to fasten him, and feeding him with everything I knew he liked. I even brought him into the house, though he was as large as a Newfoundland dog, and spread a mat for him in the corner. But his temper had really been hopelessly soured in his youth. And though I knew he was delighted in the depths of his heart when he saw me coming with his beloved lumps of sugar, he never could refrain from lifting up the corners of his mouth in that ugly snarl, and uttering his distrustful hiss, till I became quite discouraged. At last he broke his chain again and disappeared a second time.

All summer he kept himself hidden by day but crept out after sunset, foraging. And he was the terror of all the mothers who came to Appledore, and the children were watched and guarded with the greatest care lest he should find one and run away with it. But there wasn't really any reason for so much alarm. The poor bear was quite as much afraid of human beings as they could be of him.

Summer passed and winter came again and he buried himself once more in the cave on the hillside and slept till spring. But when he emerged for the second time, behold, he had waxed huge and terrible to see. With difficulty he was secured, and it was decided that now he was really dangerous and must be disposed of in some way.

About a mile and a half from Appledore lies a little island called Londoners, then occupied by a foreigner who lived there with his family. This man was found willing to take care of the bear. A price was agreed upon for his care and keep, and he was tied and put into a boat and rowed over to his new home one pleasant day in early summer, and there left and forgotten by the inhabitants of Appledore.

But in August I went over to Londoners one delicious afternoon to gather the wild pink morning glories that grew there in great abundance. I found them running all over the rocks and bushes, up elder and thistle stalks. And I carefully untwisted their strong stems and hung one vine after another over my shoulders till they fell down like a beautiful green cloak to my heels. For by carrying them in that way there was no danger of crushing or injuring the buds and rosy bells that still were open though it was afternoon. The cool sea air prevents their withering and closing as they do on the mainland and they keep open all day. I was going toward the beach with my burden, when suddenly I came upon the bear.

Oh, but he was a monster! He gave a savage growl when he saw me, an indescribable sound of hatred and wrath. And his eyes glowed red and angry. You may be sure I started back out of his reach in a flash. He was fastened by a heavy chain to a small stake. He had worn the green grass dry and dead as far as he could pace; he was huge, heavy, horrid. I came away from him as fast as I could.

As I passed near the little shanty, there ran out from the door and stood directly in my path a poor little girl six or seven years old. She was dressed in a flaming pink calico gown, and over her shoulders tumbled a thicket of dull carrot-red hair which looked as if it had never seen a comb—so dry, so rough, so knotted and tangled it was. She had small pale blue eyes and she opened her mouth and uttered some words which I vainly strove to understand. Still, she kept repeating her incantation over and over with the same monotonous tone till I really began to wonder if she were not some funny little gnome sprung up out of the earth at my feet.

I looked about. Behind me crouched the dark bulk of the angry bear. Before me in the distance I saw my friends pushing off the boat and making ready to depart. Suddenly, my ears, having grown accustomed to the savage syllables of the strange being, it flashed on me that she was saying, "Five cents for looking at the bear. Five cents for looking at the bear." precisely as if she were a machine that could do nothing else. And she never stopped saying it till I broke into hearty laughter and answered her:

"My dear Miss Caliban, I have seen the bear before. I didn't come to look at the bear. And besides, I haven't brought any money with me, or I would give you some." Upon which, she turned and hopped back with a motion and clumsiness more like a large pink toad than a human being.

Great was everybody's amusement at the idea of taxing the public for "looking at the bear." All who landed at Londoners Island, it seemed, were obliged to pay five cents for that privilege.

But the huge fellow was brought back to Appledore in September, and then his enormous strength and enormous appetite made him anything but an agreeable addition to the family. Every night, when it was quite dark and still and all the inmates of the house asleep, he prowled about, seeking what he might devour. Bolts and bars were nothing to him. Such little impediments as windows he minded not in the least, but calmly lumbered through them, taking sash, glass, and all as he came. Then he made off with everything he could find in the way of provender, and kept himself hidden all day, safely out of sight of men.

One night the family had retired early and all were wrapped in dreams. It was between ten and eleven o'clock and dark and moonless when he stole softly beneath the windows of the store-room, where were kept barrels of beef, pork, and lard, and molasses—most tempting. He climbed to one of the low windows and set his mighty shoulder against it. Crash! It gave way, and down he plunged, making noise enough to wake the dead. Two women were sleeping above in that part of the house, but they were too frightened to leave their rooms and call assistance; so they lay and trembled while our four-footed friend made himself quite at home below.

Oh, but he had a splendid time of it. He extricated great wedges of pork to carry off to his den; he wallowed into the top of the hogshead of lard till he must have been a melting spectacle; he worried the faucet out of the molasses cask and set the thick, sweet stream running all over the floor, and then rolled in it till he must have been a sugar-coated quadruped indeed. Never was a bear in such a paradise! He made expeditions to his den through the broken window, carrying off nearly a barrel of pork, and spent the greater part of the night in that blissful lake of molasses.

But when the morning dawned and the state of things below was investigated, great was the wrath and consternation in Appledore. What was to be done? Evidently this was too expensive a pet to be kept on a desert island. At this rate, he would soon dispose of all the provisions, and most likely finish off with the inhabitants in default of anything better. A dreadful decree went forth—that bear must die! He was, indeed, too dangerous in his fearful strength to be allowed to live. But to find him—there was a difficulty.

One of the men was shingling on the highest roof. He looked about him and afar off, curled in a green turfy hollow, he saw the large dark mass of Bruin's body lying like the Sybarite he was, steeping himself in sunshine after his night's orgy in the store-room. Somebody was sent out with a rifle-pistol, and before he knew that the danger was near, the sun had ceased to shine for that poor bear.

It was so instantaneous he hardly felt his death, and I was glad to know that at last all his troubles were over. But I was sorry he had ever left the wilds of Georgia to take up his abode with us at the Isles of Shoals.

ALMOST A TRAGEDY

"CHRISTINE! MAY WE COME in and see you tonight, Christine?" The children, peeping in at the kitchen door pushed it wide and danced over the threshold, delighted at the smile which greeted them.

There were three of them, Sylvia Hastings and her little brother Charlie, and Archie, a boy of fourteen at home for the winter holidays. Dearly they loved to visit Christine in her bright kitchen. And no wonder. For both the place and its occupant were most cheerful, to say nothing of the charms of Minzie, the sleek Maltese cat that lay basking on the mat in the red glow of the fire, and the absurd old gray parrot that sat muffled up in his feathers on a perch in the corner of the room. It was early dusk of the winter day, sharp and cold. A thin crisp layer of snow covered the ground without, and made the warmth and brightness within more delightful. And as for Christine, the Norwegian maid who kept the house, she was as refreshing as morning sunshine with her rosy cheeks and milk-white skin, and rich hair piled in a beautiful red-gold heap at the top of her head. The children adored her, and her employers blessed the land of Norway for having produced anything so charming and so satisfactory.

"Now, what are you doing, Christine?" asked Sylvia as they stood by the table and peered into a dull red earthen dish filled with water in which lay potatoes peeled as smooth as ivory. "What are those things, potatoes? Aren't they pretty, Archie? They look just like ivory."

"Take me up and show me!" cried little Charlie, and Archie lifted him so that he could peep too.

Christine laid a clean towel on the table, spread the potatoes on it, rolled them about in it till they were quite dry, then put them into a shallow tin pan which she had buttered, and shook them till they all shone with a thin coat of butter.

"What are they for?" asked Sylvia.

"To bake for your supper, Miss Sylvia," answered Christine.

"But why do you butter them?"

"Oh, so they may bake a lovely light brown and the skin you will not have to take off at all," answered she.

"Oh, yes I know," said Sylvia. "They are so good."

And while Christie went on with her preparations for supper, all three sat themselves down on the neat braided mat beside Minzie, the sleepy comfortable cat. She stretched her long length out slowly, and really seemed to smile at the children as she lay in the ruddy firelight with her eyes half shut, lazily responding to their caresses. She put out her paw, its sharp claws softly sheathed, and with a deprecating gesture gently patted their hands as if she were boxing her pet kitten's ears.

"Pretty Minzie." Archie said. "You are so good-natured, and you know so much."

"Good evening, good evening. Won't you take a walk?" cried a harsh voice from the corner.

"It's Polly!" cried Sylvia. "Oh, you ridiculous old bird. How you startled me!"

"What have you got in your pocket?" Polly continued, turning her head this way and that and eyeing the children askance.

"Poor Polly, not a thing," said Sylvia. "I wish I had thought to save some nuts for you."

"What does Polly want? What does Polly want?" cried the bird, and then began to utter sounds no language can describe—sounds which more nearly resembled the racket of a watchman's rattle gone distracted than anything else I can think of.

Minzie raised her head and looked toward the corner where Polly was perched and then settled comfortably back again, blinking her green eyes.

"Wise kitty," said Archie.

"Indeed she is wise," said Sylvia. "What do you think she did, Archie? When we fed the birds under the dining room window, she hid in the hedge and pounced on a bird every day, till mamma at last gave up feeding them at all, for it seemed cruel to lead them into a trap like that. Well, what does Minzie do then but steal a piece of bread from the kitchen and carry it out on the snow, and there bite it and crumble it herself, and scratch and scatter the crumbs all about. Then she hid in the hedge, the sly thing, and watched. Down came the birds, poor little hungry dears, and Minzie sprang and caught one and off she went with him to eat him up behind a bush.

"Oh, you naughty, naughty cat," continued Sylvia, lifting her finger and shaking her head at the comfortable creature, who only blinked in supreme indifference and content. "I wonder at you. How can you be so cruel?"

"But she isn't naughty, Syl," said Archie. "Cats were made to catch birds. Don't you know it?"

"Well, I wouldn't pounce on poor little birds and eat them if I were a cat," cried Sylvia.

"And I wouldn't eat little birds," said Charlie, making up a virtuous wee mouth which Sylvia stooped to kiss at once, it was so irresistable.

"But you do eat them, Syl," Archie said. "You are just as bad as Minzie."

Sylvia turned to him a shocked little face. "What do you mean, Archie?" she said.

"Why, Syl dear, didn't I see twelve small birds served up on a dish yesterday at dinner? And didn't you eat one, all but his bones? And all their claws were curled up so pitifully above them, too."

"Oh, but Archie, that's something quite different. Those birds were bought at the butcher's, you know."

"Never mind," interrupted Archie. "It is very nearly the same thing. You were made to eat some kinds of birds as well as kitty, so don't you blame her for doing what you do yourself. Don't you remember when papa was reading to mamma last night in a book called EMERSON'S ESSAYS, how astonished mamma was when he read this: 'Only the butcher stands between us and the tiger,' or something like that. And how they talked about it afterward? The cat is a little tiger. She belongs to the same family."

"Yes, I heard them talking," said Sylvia, "but I didn't understand."

"Well, never mind dear," her brother answered. "I don't think it is very easy to understand. We needn't trouble ourselves about it. Only, don't you blame poor Minzie for doing what she was made to do."

Sylvia shook her head thoughtfully. She found it a very hard riddle to read. Most of us do.

"Ship ahoy!" cried a harsh voice from the corner. "Good morning, dear. How do you do? What have you got in you pocket? Polly wants a cracker. Good gracious! Wish you happy New Year."

They all broke into laughter, Christine's merry voice mingling in the chorus.

Minzie rose from the mat, stretched herself, slowly crossed the room to where Polly sat chattering on her perch, and began to play with the chain by which the bird was fastened, giving the loop a push with her paw where it hung down, striking it every time it swung within reach. The parrot watched her meanwhile with the greatest interest. "Miaw!" cried Polly suddenly.

Minzie stopped and looked up.

"Ha,ha,ha!" shouted the bird as much as to say, "Did you think it was another cat?" and forthwith began to scream afresh, crowing like a cock, barking like a dog, imitating the creaking of a door, and then suddenly going into a frenzy of sneezing and coughing and snuffling like a person in the most desperate stages of influenza.

Minzie sat still, looking up at the bird as if she enjoyed the performance; and as for the children, they laughed till they were tired.

"Truly, they are the best of friends, the two," said Christie. "I don't know what one would do without the other. They play with each other by the hour together."

"Come, Sylvia, bring Charlie upstairs. It is time," called mamma's voice. And away the children skipped.

Christie went to and fro about her work—the pleasantest picture imaginable. I think I'll set my bread to rising before supper, she said to herself. Then I shall have more time to write my letter home this evening. So she worked fast and busily, and when the bread was made she put it in a large wooden bowl and covered it up with a nice white towel and left it to rise on the dresser. The cat and the parrot watched all these operations with an interest that amused her—it was so human.

After supper when she had done all her work and everything was in order for the night, she bade good evening to Minzie and Polly and went upstairs to write her weekly letter to her dear far-off Norway. Her room was very warm and comfortable, and as fresh and tidy as herself. She set her lamp down on the table, took out her little portfolio from the drawer, and began to write. She wrote slowly, and had been busy about an hour when she heard a loud distressed "Miaw!" outside her door. She looked up. "Miaw! Miaw! Miaw!" sounded quickly and anxiously from Minzie. Evidently something unusual was the matter. She had never heard so anxious a cry from that comfortable cat before.

"Why, what is it?" she cried as she rose and opened the door.

Minzie sprang in, apparently greatly excited, with her tail upright and curling at the top. She ran round and round Christie, rubbing herself against the girl's ankles, and looking up into her face with a most curious expression of solicitude and agitation.

"What is the matter? What is the trouble, Minzie?" Christie kept asking, as if the poor dumb creature could explain her distress in words. But Minzie only "miawed" more distractedly than before. She went toward the door, looking back at Christie, then ran to her again, took hold of her apron with her teeth, and tried to drag her toward the door. "You want me to go downstairs?"

The cat frisked before her, turning to see if she were following. Then, as if satisfied, she fled lightly and swiftly down the stairs and into the kitchen, Christie coming after, bearing the lamp in her hand. When she reached the kitchen door she heard a cry from the parrot.

"Come, come, come!" cried Polly. "Good gracious! Won't you take a walk?"

The voice did not proceed from the bird's accustomed corner, and looking about, the first thing Christie saw was the linen towel she had spread over the bread on the floor, and Minzie standing up on her hind paws with her two white-mitted forefeet at the edge of the table, craning her head forward and crying piteously.

There, in the middle of the large pan of soft dough, sat Polly sunk to her shoulders in the sticky mass, only her neck and head with its huge black beak and glassy yellow eyes to be seen. She had pulled the towel off the bread, and in the process of investigating it, had become fastened in the thick paste, sinking deeper and deeper till she was in danger of disappearing altogether.

"Ship ahoy!" cried Polly. "Come! Poor Polly! What does Polly want?"

Christine burst into laughter, and greatly to Minzi's distress, lost time in going to call Sylvia and Archie before rescuing the prisoner from her perilous position.

"Oh dear!" cried Sylvia. "How dreadful. What shall we do, Archie?"

Archie, with shouts of merriment, helped Christie disengage the poor bird and they set her into a basin of warm water to soak. She was perfectly quiet and let them do as they pleased with her, only ejaculating now and then, "Good gracious! What does Polly want? Oh, my! Won't you take a walk?" with other irrelevant remarks which sent her deliverers off into fresh peals of laughter.

"It's all very well to laugh," said Christine, "and nobody could help it. But if it had not been for Minzie, poor Polly would have been smothered in the dough and that would have been 'Good gracious!' I think."

Then she told the children how Minzie had called her, and insisted on her coming downstairs. They petted the cat and gave her no end of praise, but "Oh, you naughty bird!" cried Syl to the parrot. "Now you see what it is to meddle with things that don't concern you. Just think of it. All

Christie's nice bread must go to feed the chickens, and you came near losing your life! Don't you ever meddle again, Polly. Do you hear?"

Polly looked too comical. They had washed her as well as they could and tried to dry her, and had set her on her perch as near as they dared to the fire. She was so bedraggled and forlorn, with her wet, ruffled feathers, and her lean, shivering body. Minzie sat and looked up at her with sympathetic eyes.

"Bless my soul! What does Polly want?" chattered the poor bird.

"I should think you wanted to be punished if you weren't punished enough already," laughed Christie as she fastened the chain more securely about the parrot's leg.

Then she proceeded to make a fresh bowlful of bread in place of that which had nearly made an end of poor Polly— and presently left the two occupants of the kitchen to take care of each other till morning.

A MEMORABLE MURDER

Preface

Wedged lengthwise between Star and Appledore Islands, Smutty-Nose is one of the most barren and desolate of the Isles of Shoals. Nevertheless, a small Norwegian fishing community took hold there, and though not prosperous, they seemed to enjoy their simple life.

That is, until March 5, 1873. On this fateful evening, Karen and Anethe Christensen were brutally murdered. The violence of the act drew immediate attention to the Isles of Shoals. The islanders were beseiged with reporters looking for a scoop, investigators, and ogling tourists. The prime suspect, Louis Wagner, was taken into custody, transported by train from Boston to Portsmouth, and followed by angry mobs at every depot along the way.

Since January Celia Thaxter had been on Appledore Island with Karl nursing her invalid mother, Eliza Laighton. She hired Karen to help out, but the Norwegian woman returned to her sister Anethe and brother-in-law Ivan who were living at a cottage on Smutty-Nose.

In foul weather Celia had searched for the bodies of shipwreched sailors and even feared for her own life on more than one occasion. But this cold premeditated act of inhumanity must seriously have eroded the gentle poet's sense of trust and security in a place she always had considered a safe haven.

Thaxter's first book of prose, AMONG THE ISLES OF SHOALS, was published the same year as the murders. Because the Isles of Shoals constantly appeared in the national headlines, sales were brisk. But with the illness of her mother, Celia was overwhelmed by work and had little time to celebrate the long awaited publication.

For awhile her father, Thomas Laighton, had been an editor at *The New Hampshire Gazette,* and now she took advantage of this connection to research its news files on the murders and trial in Alfred, Maine. Piecing together factual reports and conversations with the Norwegians on the Shoals, Celia wrote a detailed account.

Only after Louis Wagner was sentenced to hang did she send the manuscript titled *A Memorable Murder* to William Dean Howells, the new editor at the *The Atlantic Monthly.* The article was accepted and appeared in the May 1875 issue of the magazine.

This is as close as Thaxter comes to objective journalism. She keeps her own viewpoints to a minimum, letting events unfold naturally and in sequence. The author relies on the use of present tense for a sense of immediacy that sets us right at the center of the blood bath. A deft use of dialogue further speeds up the narrative and engages the reader.

It is probable that Celia undertook this story as a form of catharsis. In a letter to Annie Fields, she confides that she can't help but reinact every detail of the murders in her imagination. By examining, ordering, and relegating these details to scrutiny—and then pen and paper—perhaps the sensitive young author hoped to exorcise them.

The discrepancy of the title seems to have been overlooked; there were two murders, not one. Also, one suspects the lead and closing paragraphs have been written, rewritten, and in the final analysis, overwritten. But in the main, these are minor flaws in a remarkable piece of writing. Thaxter's straightforward approach, combined with personal observation and her intimacy with the victims, is thoroughly convincing. Summer guests demanded copies. The story was widely read, and a decade later Scribner's reprinted it.

Today, the dark tale continues to be recounted by tour boat captains and retold by wide-eyed school children. It is included here in its entirety. If you are a first-time reader, hold tightly to the armchair and brace yourself for a shocking story of murder and meyhem.

A MEMORABLE MURDER

AT THE ISLES OF SHOALS, on the 5th of March in the year 1873, occurred one of the most monstrous tragedies ever enacted on this planet. The sickening details of the double murder are well known; the newspapers teemed with them for months. But the pathos of the story is not realized. The world does not know how gentle a life these poor people led, how innocently happy were their quiet days. They were all Norwegians. The more I see of the natives of this far-off land, the more I admire the fine qualities which seem to characterize them as a race. Gentle, faithful, intelligent, God-fearing human beings, they daily use such courtesy toward each other and all who come in contact with them as puts our ruder Yankee manners to shame.

The men and women living on this lonely island were like the sweet, honest, simple folk we read of in Bjornson's charming Norwegian stories, full of kindly thoughts and ways. (The murdered Anethe might have been the Eli of Bjornson's beautiful Arne or the Ragnbild of Boyesen's lovely romance.) They rejoiced to find a home just such as they desired in this peaceful place. The women took such pleasure in the little house which they kept so neat and bright, in their flock of hens, their little dog Ringe, and all

their humble belongings. The Norwegians are an exception-
ally affectionate people. Family ties are very strong and
precious among them.

Let me tell the story of their sorrow as simply as may be.

LOUIS WAGNER MURDERED ANETHE AND Karen Christensen at midnight on the 5th of March, two years ago this
spring. The whole affair shows the calmness of a practiced
hand. There was no malice in the deed, no heat. It was one
of the coolest instances of deliberation ever chronicled in
the annals of crime. He admits that these people had shown
him nothing but kindness. He says in so many words, "They
were my best friends." They look upon him as a brother. Yet
he did not hesitate to murder them.

The island called Smutty-Nose by human perversity since
in old times it bore the pleasanter title of Haley's Island was
selected to be the scene of this disaster. [The island was
called "Smutty-Nose" about two centuries prior to the arrival
of the Haley family.] Long ago I lived two years upon it,
and know well its whitened ledges and grassy slopes, its
low thickets of wild-rose and bayberry, its sea-wall still
intact, connecting it with the small island Malaga opposite
Appledore, and the ruined break-water which links it with
Cedar Island on the other side. A lonely cairn, erected by
some long ago forgotten fishermen or sailors, stands upon
the highest rock at the southwestern extremity. At its

western end a few houses are scattered—small rude dwellings, with the square old Haley house nearby. Two or three fish-houses are falling into decay about the waterside, and the ancient wharf drops stone by stone into the little cove where every day the tide ebbs and flows and ebbs again with pleasant sound and freshness. Near the houses is a small graveyard where a few of the natives sleep—and not far, the graves of the fourteen Spaniards lost in the wreck of the ship Sagunto in the year 1813. I used to think it was a pleasant place, that low rocky and grassy island, though so wild and lonely.

From the little town of Laurvig near Christiania in Norway came John and Maren Hontvet to this country, and five years ago took up their abode in this desolate spot, in one of the cottages facing the cove and Appledore. And there they lived through the long winters and lovely summers; John making a comfortable living by fishing; Maren, his wife, keeping as bright and tidy and sweet a little home for him as man could desire. The bit of garden they cultivated in the summer was a pleasure to them. They made their house as pretty as they could with paint and paper and gay pictures. And Maren had a shelf for her plants at the window. John was always so good to her; so kind and thoughtful of her comfort and of what would please her. She was entirely happy. Sometimes she was a little lonely, perhaps, when he was tossing afar off on the sea, setting or hauling his trawls, or had sailed to Portsmouth to sell his fish. So that she was doubly glad when the news came that some of her people were coming over from Norway to live with her. And first, in the month of May 1871 came her sister Karen, who stayed only a short time with Maren, and then came to Appledore where she lived at service two years till within a fortnight of her death.

The first time I saw Maren, she brought her sister to us, and I was charmed with the little woman's beautiful behavior. She was so gentle, courteous, decorous, she left on my mind a most delightful impression. Her face struck me as remarkably good and intelligent, and her gray eyes were full of light. Karen was a rather sad-looking woman, about twenty-nine years old. She had lost a lover in Norway long since, and in her heart she fretted and mourned for this continually. She could not speak a word of English at first, but went patiently about her work and soon learned enough, and proved herself an excellent servant, doing faithfully and thoroughly everything she undertook, as in the way of her people generally. Her personal neatness was most attractive. She wore gowns made of cloth woven by herself in Norway, a coarse blue stuff, always neat and clean, and often I used to watch her as she sat by the fire spinning at a spinning-wheel brought from her own country. She made such a pretty picture—with her blue gown and fresh white apron and the nice clean white muslin bow (with which she was in the habit of fastening her linen collar)—that she was very agreeable to look upon. She had a pensive way of letting her head droop a little sideways as she spun, and while the low wheel hummed monotonously, she would sit crooning sweet, sad, old Norwegian airs by the hour together, perfectly unconscious that she was affording such pleasure to a pair of appreciative eyes.

On the 12th of October 1872 in the second year of her stay with us, her brother Ivan Christensen, and his wife Anethe Mathea, came over from their Norseland in an evil day, and joined Maren and John at their island, living in the same house with them. Ivan and Anethe had been married only since Christmas of the preceding year. Ivan was tall, light-haired, rather quiet and grave. Anethe was young, fair, and merry, with thick bright sunny hair which was so long it reached (when unbraided) nearly to her knees, blue-eyes, with brilliant teeth and a clear fresh complexion. Beautiful. And beloved beyond expression by her young husband, Ivan.

Mathew Hontvet, John's brother, had also joined the little circle a year before, and now Maren's happiness was complete. Delighted to welcome them all, she made all things pleasant for them. And she told me only a few days ago, "I never was so happy in my life as when we were all living there together." So they abode in peace and quiet with not an evil thought in their minds, kind and considerate toward each other, the men devoted to their women and the women repaying them with interest—till out of the perfectly cloudless sky, one day a bolt descended without a whisper of warning, and brought ruin and desolation into that peaceful home.

LOUIS WAGNER, WHO HAD BEEN in this country seven years, appeared at the Shoals two years before the date of the murder. He lived about the island during that time. He was born in Ueckermünde, a small town of lower Pomerania in Northern Prussia. Very little is known about him, though there were vague rumors that his past life had not been without difficulties, and he had boasted foolishly among his mates that "not many had done what he had done and got off in safety." But people did not trouble themselves about him or his past, all having enough to do to earn their bread and keep the wolf from the door.

Maren describes him as tall, powerful, dark, with a peculiarly quiet manner. She says she never saw him drunk— he seemed always anxious to keep his wits about him. He would linger on the outskirts of a drunken brawl, listening to and absorbing everything, but never mixing himself up in any disturbance. He was always lurking in corners, lingering, looking, listening, and he would look no man straight in the eyes. She spoke, however, of having once heard him disputing with some sailors at table about some point of navigation. She did not understand it, but all were against Louis, and, waxing warm, all strove to show him he was in the wrong. As he rose and left the table she heard him mutter to himself with an oath, "I know I'm wrong, but I'll never give in."

During the winter preceding the one in which his hideous deed was committed, he lived at Star Island and fished alone, in a wherry. But he made very little money, and came often—over to the Hontvets where Maren gave him food when he was suffering from want, and where he received, always, a welcome and the utmost kindness.

In the following June he joined Hontvet in his business of fishing, and took up his abode as one of the family at Smutty-Nose. During the summer he was "crippled," as he said, by the rheumatism, and they were all very good to him, and sheltered, fed, nursed, and waited upon him the greater part of the season. He remained with them five weeks after Ivan and Anethe arrived, so that he grew to know Anethe as well as Maren and was looked upon as a brother by all of them, as I have said before. Nothing occurred to show his true character, and in November he left the island and the kind people whose hospitality he was to repay so fearfully. And going to Portsmouth, he took passage in another fishing schooner, the Addison Gilbert, which was presently wrecked off the coast—and he was again thrown out of employment. Very recklessly he said to

Waldemar Ingebertsen, to Charles Jonsen, and even to John Hontvet himself at different times that "he must have money if he murdered for it." He loafed about Portsmouth eight weeks, doing nothing.

Meanwhile, Karen left our service in February, intending to go to Boston and work at a sewing machine, for she was not strong and thought she should like it better than house-work. But before going, she lingered awhile with her sister Maren—fatal delay for her! Maren told me that during this time Karen went to Portsmouth and had her teeth removed, meaning to provide herself with a new set. At the Jonsens, where Louis was staying, one day she spoke to Mrs. Jonsen of her mouth—that it was so sensitive since the teeth had been taken out. And Mrs. Jonsen asked her how long she must wait before the new set could be put in. Karen replied that it would be three months. Louis Wagner was walking up and down at the other end of the room with his arms folded, his favorite attitude. Mrs. Jonsen's daughter passed near him and heard him mutter, "Three months. What is the use? In three months you will be dead." He did not know the girl was so near, and turning, he confronted her. He knew she must have heard what he said and he glared at her like a wild man.

ON THE FIFTH DAY OF March 1873, John Hontvet, his brother Mathew, and Ivan Christensen set sail in John's little schooner the Clara Bella to draw their trawls. At that time four of the islands were inhabited: one family on White Island at the lighthouse; the workmen who were building the new hotel on Star Island and one or two households besides; the Hontvet family at Smutty-Nose; and on Appledore, the household at the large house, and on the southern side opposite Smutty-Nose, a little cottage where lived Jorge Edvardt Ingebertsen, his wife and children, and several men who fished with him. Smutty-Nose is not in sight of the large house at Appledore, so we were in ignorance of all that happened on that dreadful night—longer than the other inhabitants of the Shoals.

John, Ivan, and Mathew went to draw their trawls, which had been set some miles to the eastward of the islands. They intended to be back to dinner, and then to go on to Portsmouth with their fish and bait the trawls afresh ready to bring back to set again next day. But the wind was strong and fair for Portsmouth and ahead for the islands; it would have been a long beat home against it. So they went on to Portsmouth without touching at the island to leave one man to guard the women as had been their custom. This was the first night in all the years Maren had lived there that the house was without a man to protect it. But John, always thoughtful for her, asked Emil Ingebertsen (whom he met on the fishing-grounds) to go over from Appledore and tell her that they had gone on to Portsmouth with the favoring wind, but that they hoped to be back that night. And he would have been back had the bait he expected from Boston arrived on the train in which it was due. How curiously everything adjusted itself to favor the bringing about of this horrible catastrophe! The bait did not arrive till the half past twelve train, and they were obliged to work the whole night getting their trawls ready, thus leaving the way perfectly clear for Louis Wagner's awful work.

The three women left alone watched and waited in vain for the schooner to return, and kept the dinner hot for the men, and patiently wondered why they did not come. In vain they searched the wide horizon for that returning sail. What pathos is in that longing look of women's eyes for far-off sails, that gaze so eager, so steadfast that it would almost seem as if it must conjure up the ghostly shape of glimmering canvas from the mysterious distances of sea and sky, and draw it unerringly home by the mere force of intense wistfulness. And those gentle eyes that were never to see the light of another sun looked anxiously across the heaving sea till twilight fell. And then John's messenger, Emil, arrived (Emil Ingebertsen, courteous and gentle as a youthful knight) and reassured them with his explanation, which having given, he departed leaving them in a much more cheerful state of mind.

So the three sisters, with only the little dog Ringe for a protector, sat by the fire chatting together cheerfully. They fully expected the schooner back again that night from Portsmouth. But they were not ill at ease while they waited. Of what should they be afraid? They had not an enemy in the world. No shadow crept to the fireside to warn them what was at hand, no portent of death chilled the air as they talked their pleasant talk and made their little plans in utter unconsciousness. Karen was to have gone to Portsmouth with the fishermen that day. She was already dressed to go. Various little commissions were given her, errands to do for the two sisters she was to leave behind. Maren wanted some buttons, and "I'll give you one for a pattern," she said to Karen. "I'll put it in your purse and then when you open your purse you'll be sure to remember it." (That little button of a peculiar pattern was found in Wagner's possession afterward.)

They sat up till ten o'clock, talking together. The night was bright and calm. It was a comfort to miss the bitter winds that had raved about the little dwelling all the long, rough winter. Already it was spring; this calm was the first token of its coming.

It was the 5th of March. In a few weeks the weather would soften, the grass grow green, and Anethe would see the first flowers in this strange country so far from her home where she had left father and mother, kith and kin, for love of Ivan. The delicious days of summer at hand would transform the work of the toiling fishermen to pleasure, and all things would bloom and smile about the poor people on the lonely rock. Alas, it was not to be.

At ten o'clock they went to bed. It was cold and lonesome upstairs, so Maren put some chairs by the side of the lounge, laid a mattress upon it, and made up a bed for Karen in the kitchen where she presently fell asleep. Maren and Anethe slept in the next room. So safe they felt themselves, they did not pull down a curtain nor even try to fasten the house-door. They went to their rest in absolute security and perfect trust.

It was the first still night of the new year. A young moon stole softly down toward the west. A gentle wind breathed through the quiet dark, and the waves whispered gently about the island, helping to lull those innocent souls to yet more peaceful slumber. Ah, where were the gales of March that might have plowed that tranquil sea to foam and cut off the fatal path of Louis Wagner to that happy home? But nature seemed to pause and wait for him.

I remember looking abroad over the waves that night and rejoicing over the first calm night of the year. It was so still, so bright. The hope of all the light and beauty a few weeks would bring forth stirred me to sudden joy. There should be spring again after the long winter-weariness. *Can trouble live in April days, Or sadness in the summer moons?* I thought as I watched the clear sky grown less hard than it had been for weeks, and sparkling with stars. But before another sunset, it seemed to me that beauty had fled out of the world, and that goodness, innocence, mercy, gentleness, were a mere mockery of empty words.

HERE LET US LEAVE THE poor women, asleep on the lonely rock with no help near them in heaven or upon earth, and follow the fishermen to Portsmouth, where they arrived about four o'clock that afternoon. One of the first men whom they saw as they neared the town was Louis Wagner. To him they threw the rope from the schooner, and he helped draw her in to the wharf. Greetings passed between them. He spoke to Mathew Hontvet, and as he looked at Ivan Christensen, the men noticed a flush pass over Louis' face. He asked, were they "going out again that night?" Three times before they parted he asked that question. He saw that all the three men belonging to the island had come away together; he began to realize his opportunity. They answered him that if their bait came by the train in which they expected it, they hoped to get back that night, but if it was late, they should be obliged to stay till morning baiting their trawls. And they asked him to come and help them.

It is a long and tedious business, the baiting of trawls. Often more than a thousand hooks are to be manipulated, and lines and hooks coiled clear of tangles into tubs, all ready for throwing overboard when the fishing-grounds are reached. Louis gave them a half promise that he would help them, but they did not see him again after leaving the wharf. The three fishermen were hungry, not having touched at their island where Maren always provided them with a supply of food to take with them. They asked each other if either had brought any money with which to buy bread, and it came out that every one had left his pocketbook at home. Louis, standing by, heard all this. He asked John, then, if he had made fishing pay. John answered that he had cleared about six hundred dollars.

The men parted, the honest three, about their business. But Louis, what became of him with his evil thoughts? At about half past seven he went into a liquor shop and had a glass of something, not enough to make him unsteady— he was too wise for that. He was not seen again in Portsmouth by any human creature that night. He must have gone, after that, directly down to the river—that beautiful broad river, the Piscataqua, upon whose southern bank the quaint old city of Portsmouth dreams its quiet days away. There he found a boat ready to his hand, a dory belonging to a man by the name of David Burke who had that day furnished it with new thole-pins. When it was picked up afterward off the mouth of the river, Louis' anxious oars had eaten half-way through the substance of these pins, which are always made of the hardest, toughest wood that can be found.

A TERRIBLE PIECE OF ROWING must that have been in one night! Twelve miles from the city to the Shoals—three to the lighthouses where the river meets the open sea, nine more to the islands, nine back again to Newcastle next morning. He took that boat, and with the favoring tide, dropped down the rapid river where the swift current is so strong that oars are scarcely needed, except to keep the boat steady. Truly, all nature seemed to play into his hands. This first relenting night of earliest spring favored him with its stillness. The tide was fair. The wind was fair. The little moon gave him just enough light without betraying him to any curious eyes as he glided down the three miles between the river banks—in haste to reach the sea. Doubtless the light west wind played about him as delicately as if he had been the most human of God's creatures. Nothing breathed remonstrance in his ear. Nothing whispered in the whispering water that rippled about his inexorable keel, steering straight for the Shoals through the quiet darkness.

The snow lay thick and white upon the land in the moonlight. Lamps twinkled here and there from dwellings on either side. In Eliot and Newcastle—in Portsmouth and Kittery—roofs, chimneys, and gables showed faintly in the vague light. The leafless trees clustered dark in hollows or lifted their tracery of bare boughs in higher spaces against the wintry sky. His eyes must have looked on it all, whether he saw the peaceful picture or not. Beneath many a humble roof honest folk were settling into their untroubled rest, as this planned piece of deliberate wickedness was stealing silently by, his heart full of darkness blacker than the black tide that swirled beneath his boat and bore him fiercely on.

At the river's mouth stood the sentinel lighthouses, sending their great spokes of light afar into the night, like the arms of a wide humanity stretching into the darkness—helping hands to bring all who needed succor safely home. He passed them: first the tower at Fort Point, then the taller one at Whale's Back—steadfastly holding aloft their warning fires. There was no signal from the warning bell as he rowed by, though a danger more subtle, more deadly than fog or hurricane or pelting storm was passing swift beneath it. Unchallenged by anything in earth or heaven, he kept on his way and gained the great outer ocean, doubtless pulling strong and steadily. For he had no time to lose, and the long night was all too short for an undertaking such as this.

Nine miles from the lighthouses to the island. Slowly he makes his way. It seems to take an eternity of time. And now he is midway between the islands and the coast—that little toy of a boat with its one occupant in the midst of the awful, black, heaving sea. The vast dim ocean whispers with a thousand waves. Against the boat's side the ripples lightly tap, and pass and are lost. The air is full of fine, mysterious voices of winds and waters. Has he no fear, alone there on the midnight sea with such a purpose in his

heart? The moonlight sends a long, golden track across the
waves. It touches his dark face and figure. It glitters on his
dripping oars. On his right hand Boone Island light shows
like a setting star on the horizon. Low on his left the two
beacons twinkle off Newburyport at the mouth of the Merrimack River. All the lighthouses stand watching along the
coast, wheeling their long, slender shafts of radiance as if
pointing at this black atom creeping over the face of the
planet with such colossal evil in his heart.

Before him glitters the Shoals' light at White Island,
and helps to guide him to his prey. Alas, my friendly lighthouse, that you should serve so terrible a purpose! Steadily
the oars click in the rowlocks. Stroke after stroke of the
broad blades draws him away from the lessening line of
land, over the wavering floor of the ocean, nearer the lonely rocks. Slowly the coast lights fade, and now the rote of
the sea among the lonely ledges of the Shoals salutes
his attentive ear. A little longer and he nears Appledore,
the first island, and now he passes by the snow covered,
ice-bound rock, with the long buildings showing clear in
the moonlight.

He must have looked at them as he went past. I wonder
we who slept beneath the roofs that glimmered to his eyes
in the uncertain light, did not feel, through the thick veil of
sleep, what fearful thing passed by! But we slumbered
peacefully as the unhappy women, whose doom every click

of those oars in the rowlocks, like the ticking of some dreadful clock, was bringing nearer and nearer.

Between the islands he passes. They are full of chilly gleams and glooms. There is no scene more weird than these snow covered rocks in winter, more shudderful and strange: the moonlight touching them with mystic glimmer, the black water breaking about them, and the vast shadowy spaces of the sea stretching to the horizon on every side— full of vague sounds, of half lights and shadows, of fear, and of mystery.

The island he seeks lies before him, lone and still. There is no gleam in any window. There is no help near, nothing upon which the women can call for succor. He does not land in the cove where all boats put in; he rows round to the south side and draws his boat upon the rocks. His red returning footsteps are found here next day, staining the snow. He makes his way to the house he knows so well.

ALL IS SILENT. NOTHING MOVES. Nothing sounds but the hushed voices of the sea. His hand is on the latch. He enters stealthily; there is nothing to resist him. The little dog Ringe begins to bark sharp and loud, and Karen rouses crying, "John, is that you?"—thinking the expected fishermen had returned. Louis seizes a chair and strikes at her in the dark. The clock on a shelf above her head falls down with the jarring of the blow and stops at exactly seven minutes to one.

Maren in the next room—waked suddenly from her sound sleep—trying in vain to make out the meaning of it all, cries, "What's the matter?"

Karen answers, "John scared me!"

Maren springs from her bed and tries to open her chamber door. Louis has fastened it on the other side by pushing a stick through over the latch. With her heart leaping with terror the poor child shakes the door with all her might—in vain. Utterly confounded and bewildered, she hears Karen screaming, "John kills me! John kills me!" She hears the sound of repeated blows and shrieks till at last her sister falls heavily against the door, which gives way, and Maren rushes out. She catches dimly a glimpse of a tall figure outlined against the southern window. She seizes poor Karen and drags her with the strength of frenzy within the bedroom.

This unknown terror, this fierce dumb monster who never utters a sound to betray himself through the whole, pursues her with blows, strikes her three times with a chair, (either blow with fury sufficient to kill her had it been light enough for him to see how to direct it). But she gets her sister inside and the door shut, and holds it against him with all her might—and Karen's failing strength. What a little heroine was this poor child, struggling with the force of desperation to save herself and her sisters.

All this time Anethe lay dumb, not daring to move or breathe, roused from the deep sleep of youth and health by this nameless, formless terror. Maren, while she strives to hold the door at which Louis rattles again and again, calls to her in anguish, "Anethe, Anethe! Get out of the window! Run, hide!"

The poor girl, almost paralyzed with fear, tries to obey; puts her bare feet out of the low window, and stands outside in the freezing snow, with one light garment over her cowering figure—shrinking in the cold winter wind—the clear moonlight touching her white face and bright hair and fair young shoulders.

"Scream! Scream!" shouts frantic Maren. "Somebody at Star Island may hear!"

But Anethe answers with the calmness of despair, "I cannot make a sound."

Maren screams herself, but the feeble sound avails nothing. "Run. Run!" she cries to Anethe.

But again Anethe answers, "I cannot move."

Louis has left off trying to force the door. He listens. Are the women trying to escape? He goes out-of-doors. Maren flies to the window. He comes round the corner of the house and confronts Anethe where she stands in the snow.

The moonlight shines full in his face. She shrieks loudly and distinctly, "Louis, Louis!"

Ah, he is discovered; he is recognized! Quick as thought, he goes back to the front door at the side of which stands an ax left there by Maren, who had used it the day before to cut the ice from the well. He returns to Anethe standing, shuddering there.

It is no matter that she is beautiful, young, and helpless to resist, that she has been kind to him, that she never did a human creature harm, that she stretches her gentle hands out to him in agonized entreaty crying piteously, "Oh, Louis, Louis, Louis!"

He raises the ax and brings it down on her bright head in one tremendous blow, and she sinks without a sound and lies in a heap, with her warm blood reddening the snow. Then he deals her blow after blow, almost within reach of Maren's hands, as she stands at the window.

Distracted, Maren strives to rouse poor Karen, who kneels with her head on the side of the bed. With desperate entreaty she tries to get her up and away, but Karen moans, "I cannot, I cannot." She is too far gone. And then Maren knows she cannot save her, and that she must flee herself or die. So while Louis again enters the house, she seizes a skirt and wraps it round her shoulders, and makes her way out of the open window over Anethe's murdered body—barefooted, flying away anywhere, breathless, shaking with terror.

Where can she go? Her little dog, frightened into silence, follows her—pressing so close to her feet that she falls over him more than once. Looking back, she sees Louis has lit a lamp and is seeking for her. She flies to the cove. If she can but find his boat and row away in it and get help! It is not there. There is no boat in which she can get away.

She hears Karen's wild screams—he is killing her! Oh where can she go? Is there any place on that little island where he will not find her? She thinks she will creep into one of the empty old houses by the water. But no, she reflects, if I hide there Ringe will bark and betray me the moment Louis comes to look for me. (And Ringe saved her life, for next day Louis' bloody tracks were found all about those old buildings where he had sought her.) She flies with Karen's awful cries in her ears, away over rocks and snow to the farthest limit she can gain.

The moon has set. It is about two o'clock in the morning, and oh so cold. She shivers and shudders from head to feet, but her agony of terror is so great she is hardly conscious of bodily sensation. And welcome is the freezing snow, the jagged ice and iron rocks that tear her unprotected feet, the bitter brine that beats against the shore, the winter winds that make her shrink and tremble—they are not so unkind as man's ingratitude!

Falling often, rising, struggling on with feverish haste, she makes her way to the very edge of the water. Down almost into the sea she creeps between two rocks upon her hands and knees and crouches, face downward, with Ringe nestled close beneath her breast—not daring to move through the long hours that must pass before the sun will rise again. She is so near the ocean she can almost reach the water with her hand. Had the wind breathed the least roughly, the waves must have washed over her.

THERE LET US LEAVE HER and go back to Louis Wagner. Maren heard her sister Karen's shrieks as she fled. The poor girl had crept into an unoccupied room in a distant part of the house, striving to hide herself. He could not kill her with blows, blundering in the darkness, so he wound a handkerchief about her throat and strangled her. But now he seeks anxiously for Maren.

Has she escaped? What terror is in the thought! Escaped to tell the tale, to accuse him as the murderer of her sisters. Hurriedly, with desperate anxiety he seeks for her. His time was growing short. It was not in his program that this brave little creature should give him so much trouble. He had not calculated on resistance from these weak and helpless women. Already it was morning. Soon it would be daylight. He could not find her in or near the house. He went down to the empty and dilapidated houses about the cove, and sought her everywhere.

What a picture! That blood stained butcher with his dark face, crawling about those cellars peering for that woman. He dared not spend any more time. He must go back for the money he hoped to find—his reward for this! All about the house he searches—in bureau drawers, in trunks and boxes. He finds fifteen dollars for his night's work. (Several hundreds were lying between some sheets folded at the bottom of a drawer in which he looked.) But he cannot stop for more thorough investigation. A dreadful haste pursues him like a thousand fiends.

He drags Anethe's stiffening body into the house, and leaves it on the kitchen floor. If the thought crosses his mind to set fire to the house and burn up his two victims, he dares not do it. It will make a fatal bonfire to light his homeward way. Besides, it is useless, for Maren has escaped to accuse him, and the time presses so horribly. But how cool a monster he is. After all this hard work he must have refreshment to support him in the long row back to the land.

(Knife and fork, cup and plate were found next morning on the table near where Anethe lay. Fragments of food which was not cooked in the house, but brought from Portsmouth, were scattered about. Tidy Maren had left neither dishes nor food when they went to bed. The handle of the teapot which she had left on the stove was stained and smeared with blood. Can the human mind conceive of such hideous nonchalance? Wagner sat down in that room and ate and drank. It is almost beyond belief. Then he went to the well with a basin and towels, tried to wash off the blood, and left towels and basin in the well.)

He knows he must be gone. It is certain death to linger. He takes his boat and rows away toward the dark coast and the twinkling lights. It is for dear life, now! What powerful strokes send the small skiff rushing over the water.

There is no longer any moon, the night is far spent. Already the east changes, the stars fade. He rows like a madman to reach the land. But a blush of morning is stealing up the sky and sunrise is rosy over shore and sea when—panting, trembling, weary, a creature accursed, a blot on the face of the day—he lands at Newcastle. Too late! In vain he casts the dory adrift. She will not float away. The flood tide bears her back to give her testimony against him. (And afterward she is found at Jaffrey's Point near the Devil's Den, and the fact of her worn thole-pins noted.)

Wet, covered with ice from the spray which has flown from his eager oars, utterly exhausted, he creeps to a knoll and reconnoiters. He thinks he is unobserved, and crawls on towards Portsmouth. But he is seen and recognized by many persons, and his identity established beyond a doubt. He goes to the house of Mathew Jonsen, where he has been living, steals upstairs, changes his clothes, and appears before the family, anxious, frightened, agitated, telling Jonsen he never felt so badly in his life—that he has got into trouble and is afraid he shall be taken. He cannot eat at breakfast, says "farewell forever," goes away and is shaved, and takes the train to Boston, where he provides himself with new clothes, shoes—a complete outfit. But lingering, held by fate he cannot fly, and before night the officer's hand is on his shoulder and he is arrested.

MEANWHILE, POOR SHUDDERING MAREN ON the lonely island by the waterside waits till the sun is high in heaven before she dares come forth. She thinks he may be still on the island. (She said to me, "I thought he must be there dead or alive. I thought he might go crazy and kill himself after having done all that.") At last she steals out. The little dog frisks before her. It is so cold her feet cling to the rocks and snow at every step, till the skin is fairly torn off.

Still and frosty is the bright morning. The water lies smiling and sparkling. The hammers of the workmen building the new hotel on Star Island sound through the quiet air. Being on the side of Smutty-Nose opposite Star, she waves her skirt, and screams to attract their attention. They hear her, turn and look, see a woman waving a signal of distress, and, surprising to relate, turn tranquilly to their work again. She realizes at last there is no hope in that direction. She must go round toward Appledore in sight of the dreadful house. Passing it afar off, she gives one swift glance toward it, terrified lest in the broad sunshine she may see some horrid token of last night's work. But all is still and peaceful.

She notices the curtains the three had left up when they went to bed. They are now drawn down. She knows whose hand has done this, and what it hides from the light of day. Sick at heart, she makes her painful way to the northern edge of Malaga, which is connected with Smutty-Nose by the old sea-wall. She is directly opposite Appledore and the little cottage where abide her friend and countryman, Jorge Edvardt Ingebertsen, and his wife and children. Only a quarter of a mile of the still ocean separates her from safety and comfort. She sees the children playing about the door. She calls and calls. Will no one ever hear her? Her torn feet torment her. She is sore with blows and perishing with cold.

At last her voice reaches the ears of the children, who run and tell their father that someone is crying and calling. Looking across, he sees the poor little figure waving her arms, takes his dory and paddles over, and with amazement recognizes Maren in her nightdress—with bare feet and streaming hair, with a cruel bruise upon her face, with wild eyes—distracted half senseless with cold and terror. He cries, "Maren, Maren, who has done this? What is it? Who is it?"

And her only answer is, "Louis, Louis, Louis!" as he takes her on board his boat and rows home with her as fast as he can. From her incoherent statement he learns what has happened. Leaving her in the care of his family, he comes over across the hill to the great house on Appledore.

As I sit at my desk I see him pass the window and wonder why the old man comes so fast and anxiously through the heavy snow. Presently, I see him going back again, accompanied by several of his own countrymen and others of our workmen carrying guns. They are going to Smutty-Nose and take arms, thinking it possible Wagner may yet be there. I call downstairs, "What has happened?" and am answered, "Some trouble at Smutty-Nose; we hardly understand." I say to myself, "Probably a drunken brawl of the reckless fishermen who may have landed there," and go on with my work.

In another half hour I see the men returning, reinforced by others, coming fast, confusedly, and suddenly a wail of anguish comes up from the women below. I cannot believe it when I heard them crying, "Karen is dead! Anethe is dead! Louis Wagner has murdered them both!"

I run out into the servants' quarters. There are all the men assembled, an awe-stricken crowd. Old Ingebertsen comes forward and tells me the bare facts, and how Maren lies at his house half crazy, suffering with her torn and frozen feet. Then the men are dispatched to search Appledore, to find if by any chance the murderer might be concealed about the place, and I go over to Maren to see if I can do anything for her.

I find the women and children with frightened faces at the little cottage. As I go into the room where Maren lies, she catches my hands, crying, "Oh, I so glad to see you. I so glad I save my life." And with her dry lips she tells me all the story as I have told it here.

Poor little creature, holding me with those wild, glittering, dilated eyes. She cannot tell me rapidly enough the whole horrible tale. Upon her cheek is yet the blood stain from the blow he struck with a chair, and she shows me two more upon her shoulder and her torn feet. I go back for arnica with which to bathe them. What a mockery seems to me the jocund day as I emerge into the sunshine, and looking across the space of blue sparkling water, see the house wherein all that horror lies.

Oh brightly shines the morning sun and glitters on the white sails of the little vessel that comes dancing back from Portsmouth before the favoring wind, with the two husbands on board. How glad they are for the sweet morning and the fair wind that brings them home again. And Ivan sees, in fancy, Anethe's face all beautiful with welcoming smiles, and John knows how happy his good and faithful Maren will be to see him back again. Alas, how little they dream what lies before them!

From Appledore they are signaled to come ashore. And Ivan and Mathew, landing, hear a confused rumor of trouble from tongues that hardly can frame the words that must tell the dreadful truth. Ivan only understands that something is wrong. His one thought is for Anethe. He flies to

Ingebertsen's cottage. She may be there. He rushes in like a maniac crying, "Anethe, Anethe! Where is Anethe?"

And broken-hearted Maren answers her brother, "Anethe is—at home."

He does not wait for another word, but seizes the little boat and lands at the same time with John on Smutty-Nose. With headlong haste they reach the house, other men accompanying them. There are blood stains all about the snow. Ivan is the first to burst open the door and enter. What words can tell it? There upon the floor—naked, stiff, and stark—is the woman he idolizes, for whose dear feet he could not make life's ways smooth and pleasant enough—stone dead. Dead. Horribly butchered, her bright hair stiff with blood, the fair head that had so often rested on his breast crushed, cloven, mangled with the brutal ax!

Their eyes are blasted by the intolerable sight. Both John and Ivan stagger out and fall senseless in the snow. Poor Ivan! His wife a thousand times adored, the dear girl he had brought from Norway, the good, sweet girl who loved him so, whom he could not cherish tenderly enough. And he was not there to protect her. There was no one there to save her: *Did Heaven look on, and would not take their part!*

Poor fellow, what had he done that fate should deal him such a blow as this. Dumb, blind with anguish, he made no sign: *What says the body when they spring some monstrous torture-engine's whole strength on it? No more, says the soul.*

Some of his pitying comrades lead him away like one stupefied and take him back to Appledore. John knows his wife is safe. Though stricken with horror and consumed with wrath, he is not paralyzed like poor Ivan, who has been smitten with worse than death. They find Karen's body in another part of the house, covered with blows and black in the face, strangled. They find Louis' tracks—all the tokens of his disastrous presence—the contents of trunks and drawers scattered about in his hasty search for the money. And all within the house and without, blood, blood everywhere.

When I reach the cottage with the arnica for Maren, they have returned from Smutty-Nose. John her husband is there. He is a young man of the true Norse type, blue-eyed, fair-haired, tall and well-made, with handsome teeth and bronzed beard. Perhaps he is a little quiet and undemonstrative generally, but at this moment he is superb, kindled from head to feet, a fire-brand of woe and wrath, with eyes that flash and cheeks that burn. I speak a few words to him—what words can meet such an occasion at this—and having given directions about the use of the arnica for Maren, I go away. For nothing more can be done for her, and every comfort she needs is hers.

The outer room is full of men. They make way for me, and as I pass through I catch a glimpse of Ivan crouched with his arms thrown round his knees and his head bowed down between them, motionless, his attitude expressing such abandonment of despair as cannot be described. His whole person seems to shrink, as if deprecating the blow that has fallen upon him.

All day the slaughtered women lie as they were found, for nothing can be touched till the officers of the law have seen the whole. And John goes back to Portsmouth to tell his tale to the proper authorities. What a different voyage from the one he had just taken when, happy and careless, he was returning to the home he had left so full of peace and comfort. What a load he bears back with him as he makes his tedious way across the miles that separate him from the means of vengeance he burns to reach. But at last he arrives— tells his story.

The police at other cities are at once telegraphed and the city marshal follows Wagner to Boston. At eight o'clock that evening comes the steamer Mayflower to the Shoals with all the officers on board. They land and make investigations at Smutty-Nose, then come here to Appledore and examine Maren and, when everything is done, steam back to Portsmouth—which they reach at three o'clock in the morning.

After all are gone and his awful day's work is finished at last, poor John comes back to Maren, and kneeling by the side of her bed, he is utterly overpowered with what he has passed through. He is shaken with sobs as he cries, "Oh, Maren, Maren, it is too much. Too much! I cannot bear it."

And Maren throws her arms about his neck, crying, "Oh, John, John, don't! I shall be crazy; I shall die if you go on like that."

Poor innocent, unhappy people who never wronged a fellow creature in their lives.

But Ivan—what is their anguish to his? They dare not leave him alone lest he do himself an injury. He is perfectly mute and listless. He cannot weep; he can neither eat nor sleep. He sits like one in a horrid dream. "Oh, my poor, poor brother!" Maren cries in tones of deepest grief when I speak his name to her next day. She herself cannot rest a moment till she hears that Louis is taken. At every sound her crazed imagination fancies he is coming back for her. She is fairly beside herself with terror and anxiety.

But the night following that of the catastrophe brings us news that he is arrested, and there is stern rejoicing at the Shoals. But no vengeance taken on him can bring back those unoffending lives, or restore that gentle home.

The dead are properly cared for. The blood is washed from Anethe's beautiful bright hair. She is clothed in her wedding dress—the blue dress in which she was married, poor child, that happy Christmas time in Norway a little more than a year ago. They are carried across the sea to Portsmouth; the burial service is read over them; and they are hidden in the earth.

After poor Ivan has seen the faces of his wife and sister still and pale in their coffins, their ghastly wounds concealed as much as possible, flowers upon them and the priest praying over them, his trance of misery is broken. The grasp of despair is loosened a little about his heart. Yet hardly does he notice whether the sun shines or no, or care whether he lives or dies. Slowly his senses steady themselves from the effects of a shock that nearly destroyed him, and merciful time, with imperceptible touch softens day by day the outlines of that picture at the memory of which he will never cease to shudder while he lives.

LOUIS WAGNER WAS CAPTURED IN Boston on the evening of the next day after his atrocious deed. And Friday morning, followed by a hooting mob, he was taken to the eastern depot. At every station along the route crowds were assembled, and there were fierce cries for vengeance. At the depot in Portsmouth a dense crowd of thousands of both sexes had gathered who assailed him with yells and curses and cries of "Tear him to pieces!"

It was with difficulty he was at last safely imprisoned. Poor Maren was taken to Portsmouth from Appledore on that day. The story of Wagner's day in Boston, like every other detail of the affair, has been told by every newspaper in the country: his agitation and restlessness (noted by all who saw him), his curious, reckless talk. To one he says,

"I have just killed two sailors." To another, Jacob Toldtman, into whose shop he goes to buy shoes, "I have seen a woman lie as still as that boot," and so on. When he is caught he puts on a bold face and determines to brave it out, denies everything with tears and virtuous indignation.

The men whom he has so fearfully wronged are confronted with him. His attitude is one of injured innocence. He surveys them more in sorrow than in anger, while John is on fire with wrath and indignation and hurls maledictions at him. But Ivan, poor Ivan, hurt beyond all hope or help, is utterly mute. He does not utter one word. Of what use is it to curse the murderer of his wife? It will not bring her back. He has no heart for cursing; he is too completely broken.

Maren told me the first time she was brought into Louis' presence, her heart leaped so fast she could hardly breathe. She entered the room softly with her husband and Mathew Jonsen's daughter. Louis was whittling a stick. He looked up and saw her face. And the color ebbed out of his, and rushed back and stood in one burning spot in his cheek as he looked at her and she looked at him for a space—in silence. Then he drew about his evil mind the detestable garment of sanctimoniousness, and in sentimental accents he murmured, "I'm glad Jesus loves me."

"The devil loves you!" cried John with uncompromising veracity.

"I know it wasn't nice," said decorous Maren, "but John couldn't help it. It was too much to bear."

The next Saturday afternoon when he was to be taken to Saco, hundreds of fishermen came to Portsmouth from all parts of the coast, determined on his destruction. And there was a fearful scene in the quiet streets of that peaceful city when he was being escorted to the train by the police and various officers of justice. Two thousand people had assembled, and such a furious, yelling crowd was never seen or heard in Portsmouth. The air was rent with cries for vengeance. Showers of bricks and stones were thrown from all directions, and wounded several of the officers who surrounded Wagner. His knees trembled under him. He shook like an aspen. And the officers found it necessary to drag him along, telling him he must keep up if he would save his life. (Except that they feared to injure the innocent as well as the guilty, those men would have literally torn him to pieces.)

But at last he was put on board the cars in safety and carried away to prison. His demeanor throughout the term of his confinement, and during his trial and subsequent imprisonment, was a wonderful piece of acting. He really inspired people with doubt as to his guilt. I make an extract from *The Portsmouth Chronicle*, dated March 13, 1873: "Wagner still retains his amazing *sang froid,* which is wonderful, even in a strong-nerved German. The sympathy of most of the visitors at his jail has certainly been won by his calmness and his general appearance, which is quite prepossessing." This little instance of his method of proceeding I must subjoin: A lady who had come to converse with him on the subject of his eternal salvation said, as she left him, "I hope you put your trust in the Lord," to which he sweetly answered, "I always did, Ma'am, and I always shall."

A FEW WEEKS AFTER ALL this had happened, I sat by the window one afternoon and, looking up from my work, I saw someone passing slowly—a young man who seemed so thin, so pale, so bent and ill that I said, "Here is some stranger who is so very sick he is probably come to try the effect of the air—even this early." It was Ivan Christensen; I did not recognize him. He dragged one foot after the other wearily, and walked with the feeble motion of an old man. He entered the house; his errand was to ask for work. He could not bear to go away from the neighborhood of the place where Anethe had lived and where they had been so happy, and he could not bear to work at fishing on the south side of the island, within sight of that house. There was work enough for him here. A kind voice told him so. A kind hand was laid on his shoulder and he was bidden come and welcome. The tears rushed into the poor fellow's eyes. He went hastily away and that night sent over his chest of tools—he was a carpenter by trade. Next day he took up his abode here and worked all summer.

Every day I carefully observed him as I passed him by, regarding him with an inexpressible pity of which he was perfectly unconscious—as he seemed to be of everything and everybody. He never raised his head when he answered my "Good morning," or "Good evening, Ivan." Though I often wished to speak, I never said more to him, for he seemed to me to be hurt too sorely to be touched by human hand. With his head sunk on his breast, and wearily dragging his limbs, he pushed the plane or drove the saw to and fro with a kind of dogged persistence, looking neither to the left nor right. Well might the weight of woe he carried bow him to the earth.

By and by he himself spoke to other members of the household, saying with a patient sorrow, he believed it was to have been—it had so been ordered else why did all things so play into Louis' hands? All things were furnished him: the knowledge of the unprotected state of the women, a perfectly clear field in which to carry out his plans, just the right boat he wanted in which to make his voyage, fair tide, fair wind, calm sea, just moonlight enough. Even the ax with which to kill Anethe stood ready to his hand at the house door. Alas, it was to have been!

Last summer Ivan went back again to Norway—alone. Hardly is it probable that he will ever return to a land whose welcome to him fate made so horrible. His sister Maren and her husband still live blameless lives with the little dog Ringe in a new home they have made for themselves in Portsmouth not far from the riverside. The merciful lapse of days and years takes them gently but surely away from the thought of that season of anguish. And though they can never forget it all, they have grown resigned and quiet again.

And on the island other Norwegians have settled. Voices of charming children sound sweetly in the solitude that echoed so awfully to the shrieks of Karen and Maren. But to the weirdness of the winter midnight something is added: a vision of two dim reproachful shades who watch while an agonized ghost prowls eternally about the dilapidated houses at the beach's edge close by the black whispering water, seeking for the woman who has escaped him—escaped to bring upon him the death he deserves, whom he never, never, never can find, though his distracted spirit may search till man shall vanish from off the face of the earth, and time shall be no more.

BIBLIOGRAPHY OF MAJOR WORKS
BY CELIA THAXTER

1861   "Land-locked," (First poem) *The Atlantic Monthly*

1872   POEMS New York, Hurd and Houghton.

1873   AMONG THE ISLES OF SHOALS Engravings by Harry Fenn. J.R. Osgood & Co. (28 printings)

1875   A MEMORABLE MURDER *The Atlantic Monthly;* Scribner's Anthology, 1885.

1879   DRIFT-WEED Houghton, Osgood & Co.

1883   POEMS FOR CHILDREN Houghton Mifflin Co.

1886   THE CRUISE OF THE MYSTERY And Other Poems Houghton Mifflin Co.

1894   AN ISLAND GARDEN Color illustrations by Childe Hassam. Houghton Mifflin Co. (Facsimile Edition, 1988)

1895   STORIES AND POEMS FOR CHILDREN Posthumously
        collected and edited by Sarah Orne Jewett.
        Houghton Mifflin Co.

1895   LETTERS OF CELIA THAXTER   Posthumously
        collected and edited by A.F. and R. L. (Annie
        Fields and Rose Lamb). Houghton Mifflin Co.

1896   POEMS OF CELIA THAXTER Posthumously collected
        by Sarah Orne Jewett. Appledore Edition.
        Houghton Mifflin Co.

WHAT REVIEWERS SAID THEN...

AMONG THE ISLES OF SHOALS

I think Mrs. Thaxter's prose admirable.

— *CHARLES DICKENS*

Whether the traveler goes to these isles or not, if he has this little volume, wherever he is he will have a most charming companion.

—*THE HARTFORD COURANT*

POEMS

Never before have all the wonders of our rocky New England seacoast been so musically and tenderly sung about.

—*JOHN GREENLEAF WHITTIER*

The poems seem to make something of a journal of her daily life and thought and to mark her constantly increasing power of observation.

—*SARAH ORNE JEWETT*

AN ISLAND GARDEN

It is a sort of garden idyll, notable for its thorough knowledge of flowers and seasons and birds.

—*THE NEW YORK OUTLOOK*

LETTERS

No one can read these letters without a sense of wondering affection for the rare nature they exhibit.

—*THE LITERARY WORLD*

A MEMORABLE MURDER

One of the most vivid bits of prose in American literature.

—*LAWRENCE HUTTON*

CELIA & THE SHOALS

I spent some of my pleasantest summers in the Isles of Shoals and her salon there.

—CHILDE HASSAM

Celia was "in presence what her work was: fine, frank, finished."

—WILLIAM DEAN HOWELLS

...AND NOW

Celia Thaxter died a century ago, but her writings may well be immortal.
—William Rotch, Editor
THE MILFORD CABINET

AMONG THE ISLES OF SHOALS
Her subject matter is that of poet-naturalist, and she writes as a pure local colorist determined to describe her own well-loved region.
—*LITERARY HISTORY OF THE U.S.*

POEMS
At times her austere harsh imagery anticipates poets such as Anne Sexton and Sylvia Plath . . . trying to play the many and conflictig roles of wife, mother, and artist.
—Josephine Donovan
AMERICAN WOMEN WRITERS

Her verse differs from other regional writers in that it deals chiefly with the sea, the rocks, flowers. . . Her poetry nevertheless expresses authentic content and emotion.   —Elizabeth Winslow
NOTABLE AMERICAN WOMEN

LETTERS
Struggle is revealed as part of a lively correspondence between Celia Thaxter and a few intimate friends.
—Alice Downey
A STERNE & LOVELY SCENE

AN ISLAND GARDEN
Celia Thaxter's place in the history of American gardening is clear.
—Allen Lacy
AN ISLAND GARDEN (reprint)

The revival of interest in those vibrant days has come through the publication of numerous books including Childe Hassam; An Island Garden Revisited.
—*MAINE SUNDAY TELEGRAM*

A MEMORABLE MURDER
Her prose publications remain as descriptive gems.
—*AMERICAN WOMEN WRITERS*